R00058 51422

D1083475

CHICAGO PUBLIC LIBRARY
HAROLD WASHINGTON LIBRARY CENTER

R0005851422

REF
ML
399
.S9
CIR

FORM 125 M

Music Section
Fine Arts Division

The Chicago Public Library

Received   12/27/1979

REF   MUS-BOOK

ML   Summerfield, Maurice J.
399
.S9   The Jazz Guitar.

Cop.1R   18.29

REFERENCE

REFERENCE

THE CHICAGO PUBLIC LIBRARY

MUSIC SECTION
FINE ARTS DIVISION
CHICAGO PUBLIC LIBRARY

FORM 19

THE JAZZ GUITAR

THE JAZZ GUITAR

ITS EVOLUTION

AND

ITS PLAYERS

BY

MAURICE J. SUMMERFIELD

COPYRIGHT 1978
ASHLEY MARK PUBLISHING CO.

REF
ML
399
.S9
cIR

THE JAZZ GUITAR. ITS EVOLUTION AND ITS PLAYERS. Copyright 1978 by Maurice Joseph Summerfield. All rights reserved. Printed in the United Kingdom. No part of this book may be used or reproduced in any manner whatsoever without written permission except in the case of brief quotations embodied in critical articles and reviews. For information write Ashley Mark Publishing Co. c/o Summerfield, Saltmeadows Road, Gateshead, Tyne and Wear NE8 3AJ, England.

FIRST EDITION

Typeset and printed in Great Britain by Campbell Graphics, Ltd, Newcastle upon Tyne NE1 2AR
Bound in Great Britain by Hunter & Foulis Ltd, Edinburgh
Designed by Richard Russell

ISBN 0 9506224 0 0

THE JAZZ GUITAR

CONTENTS

For my wife, Tricia

ACKNOWLEDGEMENTS

ACCENT RECORDS
ATLANTIC RECORDS

BLOOMSBURY BOOK SHOP
BLUE BAG RECORDS

CBS RECORD CO.
TOM CHARLTON
TERESA CHILTON
GEORGE CLINTON
ALAN M. COLLINS
CONCORD JAZZ INC.
CRESCENDO MAGAZINE
JIM CROCKETT

CHARLES DELAUNAY

DOWN BEAT MAGAZINE

ENJA RECORDS
ECM RECORDS

LEONARD FEATHER
FAMOUS DOOR RECORDS

IZYDOR GEFFNER
GUILD GUITARS
GUITAR MAGAZINE
GUITAR PLAYER MAGAZINE

IBANEZ GUITARS

JAZZ CHRONICLES RECORDS
JAZZ JOURNAL

PETE LARTER
NEIL LILIEN

MARIO MACCAFERRI
MELODY MAKER
MONMOUTH EVERGREEN RECORDS
DENNIS MATTHEWS

MARCUS PRICE
PABLO RECORDS

CHARLES E. H. SMITH
TONY SMITH
NEVILLE SKRIMSHIRE
JIMMY STEWART

VANGUARD RECORDS

WARNER BROS. RECORDS
VALERIE WILMER
JIMMY WYBLE
W. G. WOONINCK

XANADU RECORDS

PREFACE

For over twenty years I have waited for someone to produce a book which comprehensively covers the subject of the jazz guitar. Despite the fact that many books have been written on jazz history, its personalities, and jazz in general, the guitar's involvement with this form of music has not really been dealt with in any depth. The total output to date seems to be two books on Django Reinhardt, selected chapters in a few books, several good magazine articles, two discographies of Charlie Christian, and a soft bound collection of interviews with jazz guitarists orginally printed in 'Guitar Player' magazine.

I therefore decided two years ago to take the 'bull by the horns' and write a book on the jazz guitar—its evolution and its players. I thought then that the project would take me six months but in fact it has taken over two years. When I originally wrote several articles for the English magazine 'Guitar' entitled 'The World of Jazz Guitar', I was then surprised by the amount of correspondence I received. It was obvious that many guitarists wanted to know more about the jazz guitar. I am also frequently amazed that many of the fine guitar players in other fields of music whom I meet are ignorant of much of the work of the great jazz guitarists. These facts have inspired and encouraged me to complete the work.

The finished product is now before you and the contents are based upon my involvement with and love of jazz, and the jazz guitar, for over twenty years. One of the most important features of the book is its very full listing of records, music, methods and books by jazz guitarists. Many of the items listed are still currently in production or print, those which are not can be obtained with a little patience by using the section, 'Sources of Supply', at the back of the book. I have personally found that an advert placed in one or more of the specialist magazines will often bring that elusive item. You will also be amazed, particularly if you live in a larger city, at what your local main library can offer. In regard to records you should remember that many items are available in different countries with different brands, sleeves, and numbers, so be careful not to duplicate or be misled.

The collection of photographs in this book of jazz guitarists, past and present, is I believe a unique one. I personally have great pleasure in seeing such a collection under one cover and I wish to give special thanks to all those who have supplied them. Their contribution has been vital for the excellent illustration of the book.

I realize there is a possibility that some readers of this book may find that one or more of their favourite jazz guitarists have not been included. However I have sincerely tried to include all those players who I believe have made an impact on the evolution of the guitar in jazz since 1895. I personally enjoy and admire the wonderful guitar playing of country artists Chet Atkins, Jerry Reed and Glen Campbell, and also studio guitarists Tony Motolla and Al Caiola. Nevertheless they are not included in this book as I do not class them as jazz musicians. I am also aware that there are many fine guitarists throughout the world who are capable of playing good jazz but circumstances and events have not allowed them to contribute in a really effective way to date. Some of these that I have heard or know of are illustrated in the appendix to the players' section as a tribute to their ability and love of jazz.

MAURICE J. SUMMERFIELD 1978

THE JAZZ GUITAR

ITS EVOLUTION

THE EVOLUTION OF THE JAZZ GUITAR

		In the U.S.A.	*Outside the U.S.A.*
1895	**The Blues**	†Big Bill Broonzy/Leadbelly Blind Willie McTell/Blind Lemon Jefferson	
1900	**New Orleans**		
1910	**Dixieland** **Chicago**	THE ⎱ Bud Scott BANJO ⎰ Johnny St Cyr Snoozer Quinn *Eddie Lang/*Lonnie Johnson	
1930	**Kansas City**	*Carl Kress/*Dick McDonough *George Van Eps/Teddy Bunn Freddie Green (rhythm guitar) Allan Reuss	*Django Reinhardt Oscar Aleman
1940	**Swing**	Al Casey/Tiny Grimes *Charlie Christian Oscar Moore/George Barnes/Les Paul	
1945	**Be Bop**	*Barney Kessel *Tal Farlow/*Chuck Wayne	
1950	**Modern/West Coast**	*Jimmy Raney/Herb Ellis Jim Hall	René Thomas
	Cool	Billy Bauer/Johnny Smith Kenny Burrell/*Wes Montgomery	
1960	**Bossa/Nova**	*Laurindo Almeida/Charlie Byrd *Joe Pass/George Benson	Baden Powell Attila Zoller Gabor Szabo
1970	**Avant Garde** Jazz/Rock/Soul Indo/African/Free	Larry Coryell/Al Di Meola Lee Ritenour	*John McLaughlin Derek Bailey

†These artists' recordings give a true representation of the music of the blues singer/guitarists of this period.

*THE MAJOR INNOVATORS

A chart showing those guitarists who have had an important influence on the evolution of the jazz guitar from the beginning of jazz music to the present day.

THE JAZZ GUITAR

ITS EVOLUTION

Many books have been written about the origins of jazz. The authors have varying concepts and theories about these origins but most agree that the beginnings of jazz, as we know it today, happened about 1895. Few would disagree that the guitar, albeit in many cases in a primitive form, was the first instrument of jazz. The first organized jazz began in the form of marching bands in New Orleans and a photograph of the earliest known jazz group, Buddy Bolden's band from about 1894, shows a guitarist as part of the line-up. The early negro blues singers, prior to and after 1895, used the guitar for their accompaniment. Those singer/guitarists who had developed their technique on the instrument were able to interject their accompaniments with single note lines and riffs to add colour and impetus to their performance. Although we obviously have no recorded proof of what these artists sounded like there seems little doubt that the records made later by singer/guitarists such as Big Bill Broonzy, Leadbelly, and Blind Willie McTell give us a true representation of the first sounds of jazz and the jazz guitar.

As a real solo voice in its own right the guitar was to become eventually one of the last instruments of jazz. This was mainly due to the guitar's lack of volume and carrying power. Until the arrival of microphones, recording, and the first primitive amplification in the mid-nineteen twenties the guitar was relegated to the rhythm section in organized jazz, felt rather than heard. The banjo, because of its bright, loud and cutting sound was the preferred instrument in early jazz groups, although the guitar was still the primary instrument used for accompaniment by blues singers. There were important jazz artists such as Bud Scott, often heard with Kid Ory, and Johnny St Cyr who played with Louis Armstrong, who doubled on both banjo and guitar, but their prime role was as part of the rhythm section.

The first jazz guitarist who could solo in an articulate manner, comparable to performers on other instruments of jazz, was the negro blues singer Lonnie Johnson. He was featured as a backing artist on many records in the mid-nineteen twenties and was a soloist on a 1928 recording by Duke Ellington and his orchestra entitled 'The Mooche'. Johnson had early musical training on the violin and there seems little doubt that this training combined with his special natural musical talents made him aware of the single note capabilities of the guitar as a solo voice. There is also no

Brock Mumford, guitarist with Buddy Bolden's Jazz Band, circa 1894.

doubt that it was Johnson's playing that directly inspired Eddie Lang the brilliant white guitarist from Philadelphia, who incidentally also had an early training on the violin. Lang picked up the blues style of Johnson's guitar playing very quickly, and was able to reach international fame within a relatively short period of time. Fame that the coloured artist Johnson could not have access to then due to racial prejudice. Yet Lang fully realized the genuine talents of Johnson and not only played with him in private but recorded several ageless guitar duos with him, often under the pseudonym of Blind Willie Dunn.

Many of these recordings made by Johnson and Lang, both their solos and duos, are now fortunately available once more and bear full testimony to the greatness of both guitarists. Lang was a virtuoso of the guitar and was able to mix authentic blues lines with long and exciting flowing arpeggios, chords and runs. His guitar was often heard with the other jazz masters of the twenties including Bix Beiderbecke and Joe Venuti. From 1929 Lang was also a prominent voice with the Paul Whiteman orchestra. The only other guitarist of note of the late twenties was Snoozer Quinn. He had a fine reputation amongst jazzmen in the New York area but due to illness and other reasons never achieved lasting fame. Eddie Lang at the height of his career, having become the full time accompanist of his friend the singer Bing Crosby,

Dick McDonough

died suddenly in 1932 as a result of a tonsillectomy. His death was a tragic loss that held up the evolution of the jazz guitar in the U.S.A. for a while.

Carl Kress, Dick McDonough, and George Van Eps stand out as being the most important jazz guitarists in America during the early thirties, particularly after the death of Eddie Lang. They were great rhythm guitarists and their solo style was a happy mixture of single note lines and punchy, rhythmic chords, a derivation of the solo banjo style developed in jazz bands during the twenties. Kress, McDonough and Van Eps were all originally banjoists. Coloured guitarist Teddy Bunn, featured with the vocal group 'The Spirits of Rhythm', continued and extended the blues influenced guitar style of Lonnie Johnson.

But it was to Europe that jazz lovers turned their attention when the everlasting genius of Django Reinhardt exploded on the scene in 1934. Django, a Belgian-born gypsy, had overcome a terrible disability. virtually the total loss of the use of his third and fourth fingers of his left hand. This occurred after a fire in his caravan in 1928. He developed a new technique which enabled him to portray fully on the guitar his fantastic mixture of improvised music, fired by both his gypsy background and his love for the American jazz that he had heard on early records. His virtuoso guitar

Bud Scott

14

Eddie Lang with the Mound City Blue Blowers.

COURTESY C. E. H. SMITH

playing carried to new high levels the standards of solo jazz guitar playing which had been set by Eddie Lang. His artistry virtually overshadowed American jazz guitarists of that time, particularly after the early death of Dick McDonough in 1938.

Prior to Lang and Johnson the guitar had been an integral part of the rhythm section in many jazz bands. This tradition, started by artists such as Johnny St Cyr and Bud Scott was continued into the thirties and forties by two men in particular, Eddie Condon and Freddie Green. Eddie Condon, who played a four string guitar (an instrument which facilitated the changeover to guitar for early banjo players) through the years until his death in 1973, was one of the greatest promoters of Chicago style jazz. The amazing Freddie Green has for the past forty years been the pulse and the driving force of the legendary Count Basie band. He has, and continues to, set unsurpassed standards in the art of the rhythm guitar.

The next important step in the evolution of the jazz guitar was to come in 1939 when jazz promoter John Hammond discovered the Oklahoma born guitarist Charlie Christian. Christian's genius in a very short period of time opened new horizons for not only the guitar but for jazz itself. But it was most certainly the inventive and enquiring mind of trombonist/guitarist/arranger Eddie Durham that speeded the

transformation of the acoustic guitar to its amplified state. Durham had experimented for a few years with amplifying the guitar. At first he tried attaching a resonator to his instrument and with this device recorded the attractive 'Hittin the Bottle' with Jimmy Lunceford in 1935. In 1937 whilst working with the Count Basie band on trombone, Durham played and recorded with a small group out of the band, the Kansas City Six, on one of the first electric guitars. It was Durham who made Charlie Christian aware of the electric guitar as early as 1937. The young negro guitarist quickly realized the potential which the electric guitar offered. He saw that notes could be sustained, and a saxophone style of single note playing which he so admired could be obtained, and of course the volume of the guitar could now equal any other instrument. In fact many early observers of Christian's playing actually thought at first they were listening to a saxophone. As the nineteen forties approached there were other fine jazz guitar soloists making their mark, but they were mainly acoustic guitar players. Al Casey with Fat Waller's sextet and Allan Reuss with the Benny Goodman and Jack Teagarden bands are amongst the best of these. But it was the combination of the amplified guitar and Christian's advanced and brilliant harmonic concepts that suddenly opened the doors wide, not only for the jazz guitar, but for jazz itself. On the recommendation of John Hammond, Charlie was hired by Benny Goodman

Guitarmen, Wake Up and Pluck!

Wire for Sound; Let 'Em Hear You Play

BY CHARLIE CHRISTIAN
(Featured Guitarist, Benny Goodman Orchestra)

Guitar players have long needed a champion, someone to explain to the world that a guitarist is something more than just a robot plunking on a gadget to keep the rhythm going. For all most bandleaders get out of them, guitarists might just as well be scratching washboards with sewing thimbles.

There are dozens of guitar players around the country—and I mean *good* guitar players—who have resigned themselves to a life of playing for nothing but cookies or just their own kicks, because they've had no alternative if they wanted to continue playing guitar.

Bernard Addison, formerly with Stuff Smith's band, in the August '39 DOWN BEAT, said:

Git-men Get Short End

"Guitarists are goats. In the present day band's setup, it's the guitar player who gets the short end. Leaders don't appreciate the possibilities of the instrument."

I've been inclined to agree 100 per cent with Addison, although

CHARLIE CHRISTIAN
Thinks amplification gives guitarists new lease on life.

naturally there are leaders who have been exceptions to this generality (and not out of fear for my job do I say that Benny is one of them).

With an appalling ignorance of the effective use to which they could put the instrument, most leaders, including those in the radio and movie studios, have demanded a guitarist who can fiddle, arrange or pick his teeth walking a tight rope every other chorus. The fact that he might have been truly an artist on the guitar was negligible.

A New Era Dawning

And arrangers seem either to have neglected to learn anything about the guitar or else have found that arranging for it is beyond their ability.

But the dawn of a new era is at hand for all these fine guitarists who had become resigned to playing to feed their souls but not necessarily their stomachs.

Electrical amplification has given guitarists a new lease on life.

Allan Reuss, with Jack Teagarden's band, was one of the first well-known men to attach an amplifier to his guitar. Musicians have been aware of Reuss's ability for several years, but the instrument is subtle and the public probably never would have realized his ability if they'd had to strain their ears to catch the niceties of his technique and the beauty of his improvisations. Allan's recent work on Jack Teagarden's Brunswick record, *Pickin' for Patsy*, his own number, proved to the record companies as well as to musicians and public alike that as a solo jazz instrument the guitar is far from stillborn. Reuss's guitar was amplified on the session.

Smith Gains Prominence

Then there's Georgie Barnes, the 17-year-old Chicagoan, who, with an amplified instrument, set that town on its ear at Chicago's Off-Beat club last spring. Barnes has just been added to the staff of the Chicago NBC studios. A year ago he had a tough time booking his own Chicago Heights combo for Saturday nights.

And Floyd Smith, the colored guitar player with Andy Kirk's band. With an amplified guitar he has been acclaimed widely as one of the greatest guitarists of all time, particularly in the blues idiom. His work on the Decca record, *Floyd's Blues*, with the Kirk band, forces his ability and the value of the guitar smack into the consciousness and ears of the public.

Needless to say, amplifying my instrument has made it possible for me to get a wonderful break. A few weeks ago I was working for beans down in Oklahoma and most of the time having a plenty tough time of getting along and playing the way I wanted to play.

Practice Solo Stuff

So take heart, all you starving guitarists. I know and so does the rest of our small circles, that you play damned fine music, but now you've got a chance to bring the fact to the attention of not only short-slighted leaders but to the attention of the world. And I don't think it'll be long before you're feeding your stomach again as well as your heart. Practice solo stuff, single string and otherwise, and save up a few dimes to amplify your instrument.

You continue to play guitar the way it should be played and you'll make the rest of the world like it.

Johnny Dodds is Slowly Recovering

Chicago — Johnny Dodds, early day New Orleans jazz clarinet player, who was stricken with a severe illness in August, is slowly recovering at his home on the south side here. According to his

When Bix Was with Goldkette in 1927

these pictures were taken for Red Ingle, who also was with the band at the same time. Picture on the left, taken at Castle Farms, Cincinnati, shows Bix and Ingle (who now is with Ted Weems' band in Chicago). The shot of Bix on the right was taken later the same year, outside a spot the band played on the shores of Lake Erie at Fremont, Ohio. (Photos courtesy of Ingle).

in 1939 and was featured as a main soloist with Goodman's big band and sextet.

In the same way that banjo players at the beginning of the thirties changed virtually en masse to the guitar, the beginning of the forties saw a mass changeover from the acoustic to the electric guitar. The nineteen thirties heralded the big band era and the boom of swing music. The early part of the decade saw guitarists like McDonough, Kress and Van Eps fitting into the big band scene in a relatively subordinate role, despite their genuine virtuoso talent on the instrument. We are fortunate that some of these artists' outstanding solos and duets are once more available on record. Their style of playing was carried on by other white guitar players such as Carmen Mastren and Allan Reuss, and in a more blues influenced way by the coloured artist Al Casey. These guitarists were virtually unaffected by the continental style of jazz being played at that time in Europe by Django Reinhardt, and to a lesser extent by Argentinian born Oscar Aleman. We do know that Charlie Christian greatly admired Django, and would often play the gypsy's recorded solos note for note when playing in jazz clubs in Oklahoma and New York.

After joining Goodman, Christian tragically lived for only a little more than two years but in that time he transformed the position of the guitar in jazz. The style and ideas that he had developed set new standards for jazz that were unsurpassed for many years to come.

The early forties saw national prominence for two guitarists from Chicago, one was Les Paul, a great Django Reinhardt fan, and the other George Barnes, who attributed his distinctive style to various reed players rather than guitarists. Les Paul was one of the first guitarists to experiment with the development of the electric guitar and in fact played an amplified instrument as early as 1937.

Charlie Christian

Both Paul and Barnes were really not affected by Christian but virtually all the other new guitarists to come to the fore in the forties were. Oscar Moore, and later Irving Ashby and John Collins with the Nat King Cole trio were all inspired by Charlie Christian. The only female guitarist ever to make an impression on the jazz scene, Mary Osborne, was also a Christian devotee particularly after she had met and befriended him.

With the success of Benny Goodman's big band and small groups, most other big bands were anxious to have an electric guitarist in order to try and achieve the same type of success. In 1944 the great jazz promoter Norman Granz produced his film 'Jammin' the Blues' which featured many of the top jazz stars of the day. The only white musician to be featured in this film was a twenty-one-year-old guitarist from Muskogee, Oklahoma called Barney Kessel. Like Mary Osborne he had also met and befriended Charlie Christian. Kessel's driving, blues influenced style of guitar, so obviously an authentic extension of Christian's playing, was recognized by many jazz critics as making him the true successor to Charlie Christian. For the next few years, right up to his entry into the Hollywood studios in the mid-fifties, Barney Kessel was generally regarded as the leading jazz guitarist in the United States of America.

As the nineteen fifties approached a multitude of fine jazz guitarists were developing on both coasts of North America. They set standards which were virtually unsurpassed by any guitarists outside America for many years, with the exception of Django. Particularly prominent were Tal Farlow,

Teddy Bunn (bottom left) with the Spirits of Rhythm

Jimmy Raney, Jim Hall and Herb Ellis, Mundell Lowe, Johnny Smith, Chuck Wayne, Billy Bauer, and Sal Salvador. These and many other American guitarists were fortunate that important small groups led by other jazz instrumentalists were to prove valuable training grounds for the development of their skills on the guitar. Vibist Red Norvo, Pianists—Nat King Cole, Art Tatum, Oscar Peterson, George Shearing, Drummer—Chico Hamilton, Saxophonists—Stan Getz, Jimmy Giuffre were probably the most important of these. The first hints of avant garde jazz were intimated at that time by a group led by saxophonist Lee Konitz, pianist Lennie Tristano and guitarist Billy Bauer. In Europe Django Reinhardt still reigned supreme, his natural musical genius effortlessly absorbed and accepted all the new movements and changes in jazz.

The stage was now set for a new development in the evolution of the jazz guitar. The amplified guitar had enabled Christian and his followers to put their instrument on an equal footing with all other single note instruments in jazz. The acoustic 'F' hole guitar was also often still used as an essential part of the rhythm section playing four in the bar, straight chords. But the power of amplification for a time had made many guitarists forget that the guitar was more than a single note instrument. They were quite content to play long flowing single note lines, many in the manner of

Django Reinhardt and Barney Kessel 1953

saxophonists Lester Young and Charlie Parker, neglecting many other aspects of the guitar. In California during the late forties, George Van Eps, who had come to prominence with several big bands in the thirties, was still fascinated by the overall harmonic possibilities that the guitar offered. Even though he was using an acoustic guitar as late as 1949 his recorded solos during this period show that he had an amazingly modern harmonic concept of music. He also had an incredible technique to display these concepts with. He showed that the guitar could solo not only with single notes, but in a piano like manner with a mixture of chords, octaves, double notes and single notes.

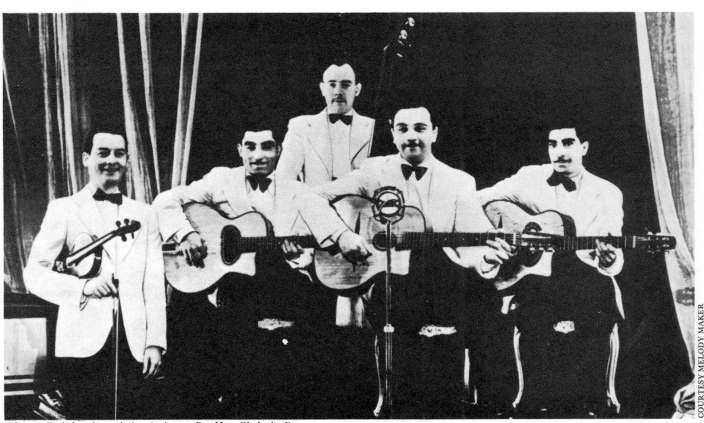

Django Reinhardt and the Quintet Du Hot Club de France

COURTESY MELODY MAKER

Charlie Byrd

Van Eps' playing obviously influenced the 'heir' to Charlie Christian's throne, Barney Kessel. Kessel suddenly realized that he had the ability and the desire to play his own individual style of jazz rather than a replica of the patterns laid down by Christian. He also saw that the guitar was really a 'small orchestra' and that in a small group form it could only display its full capabilities by deleting the piano. His experiments finally led to the first recording in 1957 of his group 'The Poll Winners', which was made up of himself on guitar, Ray Brown on bass, and Shelly Manne on drums. This recording and others that followed were a great success and the format of the group, although a very standard form today for guitar players, was a great innovation at that time. Kessel proved that if a guitarist had the right technique, concepts and talent, the guitar could fill the role of soloist and accompanist as on the piano, and so give the guitar a freedom of performance and expression previously unknown.

In 1953 at the age of forty-three Django Reinhardt died suddenly of a heart attack in France. Fortunately his music was to live on for all over the world groups have continued to emulate his music and the sound of the quintet of the Hot Club de France. In 1953 in America a new sound was being added to the repertoire of the jazz guitar. Brazilian born guitarist Laurindo Almeida, who had come several years earlier to the United States to play with the Stan Kenton orchestra, conceived of the idea of mixing traditional Brazilian melodies and rhythms with jazz improvisations. His group 'Brazilliance' co-led with saxophonist Bud Shank, featured Laurindo on the classical guitar. With the use of high quality microphones and amplifiers Laurindo proved that the nylon strung, finger style instrument could be an effective sound in jazz. He also showed that the horizons of jazz music could be broadened further with the introduction of South American melodies and rhythms. The Brazilliance group received quite a lot of popular success but its conception was premature. It took another finger style guitarist, Charlie Byrd to pick up and succeed on a grand scale what Laurindo Almeida had started. Byrd, who had successfully played his own style of jazz on the classical guitar had been chosen by the State Department to go with his trio to South America. Whilst he was there Byrd realized the potential of mixing several popular Brazilian songs by composer/guitarists such as Antonio Carlos Jobim and Luiz Bonfa with jazz. On his return to the United States in 1961 Byrd joined forces with saxophonist Stan Getz and together they helped begin the bossa nova boom with songs like 'Desafinado'. 'O Pato', and 'Girl from Ipanema', which eventually swept the world. The success of Bossa Nova, brought to the attention of the world's jazz lovers the talents of other South American guitarists, such as Bola Sete and Baden Powell.

By the beginning of the nineteen sixties jazz and the jazz guitar had for many years prospered and enjoyed great popularity. But jazz was now generally in decline and many top line jazz guitarists had to take financial refuge in the film, television and recording studios. The rise of rock and roll, with few exceptions, stunted the growth

Joe Pass

19

of jazz for some time to come. Nevertheless the jazz guitar had never had so many great and individual instrumentalists. There was the main stream directly stemming from Charlie Christian which had wonderful artists such as Barney Kessel, Jimmy Raney, Tal Farlow, Kenny Burrell, Grant Green, Jim Hall and Herb Ellis. The rhythm guitar tradition was still maintained by artists like Freddie Green whilst finger style guitarists such as Charlie Byrd and Bola Sete were adding new dimensions to jazz on the classical guitar. Johnny Smith's record of 'Moonlight in Vermont' with Stan Getz had been a best seller and his virtuoso technique and block chording made guitarists rethink. George Van Eps made new inroads with his development of the electric seven string guitar which were taken up later by Bucky Pizzarelli, and at the same time blues singer/guitarists like Lonnie Johnson were once more in demand.

It was a coloured guitarist from Indianapolis called Wes Montgomery who gave the jazz guitar a much needed shot in the arm in 1960. Wes had developed an individual warm guitar sound by using the thumb of his right hand instead of a pick. His solos never lost interest due to a happy and wonderful mixture of chords, long flowing lines of single notes, and an unusually articulate use of octaves. His solo style was so attractive that his later records were sold en masse to the popular market. Montgomery also started a new wave of jazz guitarists emulating the guitar style which he had originated. The most important of these were Pat Martino and George Benson. Fate over the years had already dealt the evolution of the jazz guitar

Freddie Green

COURTESY JAZZ JOURNAL/PHOTO T. H. ADKINS

severe blows with the early deaths of Eddie Lang at 29, Charlie Christian at 23, Dick McDonough at 34 and Django Reinhardt at 43. It decided in its own way also to take Wes Montgomery at the age of 44. But like all other legendary giants of the jazz guitar Wes had left a deep and lasting mark in jazz history, one that will never be forgotten.

By the end of the nineteen sixties the jazz guitar had certainly come a long way since the primitive blues singer/guitarists of the late nineteenth century. Standards had been set on this most difficult of all instruments that had never been conceived of at the beginning of the century. The incredible rise world-wide in the popularity of Rock and Roll, Soul and Rhythm and Blues music in the sixties on the one hand had caused a temporary decline in the popularity of jazz. On the other hand vast numbers of people were being attracted to the guitar and other instruments because of their interest in popular music. Many of these progressed technically to such a stage that they sought for a style of music that offered them qualities that could not be found in the basic forms of popular music. As the nineteen seventies approached a new world-wide boom in jazz began.

This boom has allowed the great jazz guitar masters of the fifties and sixties, such as Barney Kessel, Tal Farlow, Jimmy Raney, Herb Ellis, Kenny Burrell, Jim Hall to leave the commercial studios or virtual retirement. They are once more successfully playing all over the world in jazz clubs, concerts and festivals, setting standards that are pushing the boundaries of the jazz guitar to even wider limits. Standing by the side of these masters are a new breed of young guitarists who, although versed

George Benson

COURTESY IBANEZ GUITARS

in all the earlier styles of jazz, are deeply affected by the whole spectrum of modern music—Avant Garde, Rock, Soul, Latin, Indian, African, Oriental, Arab and Free music. So today we have many new jazz guitarists whose playing is affected by all these idioms. Larry Coryell, John McLaughlin, John Abercrombie, and Lee Ritenour are only a few of the major figures adding new dimensions to jazz and the jazz guitar in the seventies. An English guitarist Derek Bailey is one of the prime instigators of the movement of free jazz, a movement which is gaining an ever increasing audience throughout the world. These young men are all conscious of the established jazz greats but feel that they must strive for fresh ideas in jazz, ideas as yet unheard of. In the midst of all these artists striving for new limits in jazz we have seen over the last few years the rise of Joe Pass. This amazing guitarist, a continuation of the mainstream of jazz guitar, came to light in the early sixties but his genius was only fully recognized then by jazz promoter Norman Granz. Over the past few years, through records and concerts, Granz has managed to make the world aware of Joe's virtuoso ability on the guitar. Joe has, like most of the great jazz men, developed his own style on the foundations of earlier jazz artists. But today he has evolved an incredible and individual technique that allows him to play concerts totally on his own, setting once again new standards in the field of jazz guitar.

As the nineteen eighties approach the world of the jazz guitar is certainly a wonderful one, and one that has never been so varied. Side by side virtually every aspect of the jazz guitar is prospering throughout the world. Record companies are re-issuing as quickly as possible every old jazz recording of worth that they have, and jazz guitar enthusiasts can buy records of most of the all time jazz greats, study and learn from them. There seems no doubt that the nineteen eighties will be the most exciting period that jazz has known, a period in which the role of the guitar will contribute even more to the development of jazz than it has done to date.

Wes Montgomery

COURTESY JAZZ JOURNAL/PHOTO MICHAEL SALTER

SELECTED BOOKS—for an appreciation of the history of jazz and the jazz guitar.

'The Book of Jazz'	Leonard Feather—Horizon	1957
'The Encyclopedia of Jazz'	Leonard Feather—Horizon	1960
'The Encyclopedia of Jazz of the Sixties'	Leonard Feather—Horizon	1967
'The Encyclopedia of Jazz of the Seventies'	Feather/Gitler—Horizon	1976
'The Jazz Book'	Joachim Berendt—Paladin	1976
'Jazz Masters of the Twenties'	R. Hadlock—McMillan/Collier	1966
'Jazz Masters of the Forties'	Ira Gitler—McMillan/Collier	1966
'Jazz Masters of the Fifties'	J. Goldberg—McMillan/Collier	1965
'Jazz Masters of the Transition 1957—69'	Martin Williams—McMillan/Collier	1966
'Jazz Masters of New Orleans'	Martin Williams—McMillan/Collier	1967
'Who's Who of Jazz'	John Chilton—Chilton Book Co.	1970
'Jazz Now'—edited Roger Cotterrell	Jazz Centre Society—Quartet Book	1976
'A Pictorial History of Jazz'	Keepnews Graver—Spring Books	1959
'Esquire's World of Jazz'	L. W. Gillenson—A Barker Co.	1963
'Combo U.S.A.'	Rudi Blesh—Chilton Book Co.	1971
'The Devils Music—History of the Blues'	Oakley—BBC Publications	1976
'Shining Trumpets'	Rudi Blesh—Cassell	1958
'Early Jazz'	Gunther Schuller—Oxford University Press	1968
'The Story of Jazz'	Marshall Stearns—Oxford University Press	1958
'Jazz Guitarists'	Guitar Player Productions	1975
'Modern Jazz'	Morgan & Horricks—Gollancz	1957
'The Art and Times of the Guitar'	Grunfeld—McMillan	1969
'Guitars'	Tom and Ann Mary Evans—Paddington	1977

'Jazz Hot'—May 1972 is devoted entirely to jazz guitarists and the jazz guitar (in French)

SELECTED RECORDS—for a general appreciation of jazz guitar over the years.

'Pioneers of the Jazz Guitar'		Yazoo	L—1057
'Fifty Years of Jazz Guitar	(2 lp's)	Columbia	CG 33566
'The Jazz Guitar Album'	(2 lp's)	Verve	2683—065
'Guitar Player'	(2 lp's)	MCA	MCA 2—6002

John Abercrombie and Ralph Towner (right).

COURTESY GUILD GUITARS

'down beat' MAGAZINE READER'S POLL WINNERS 1936–77 — GUITAR

1936	Eddie Lang	1957	Barney Kessel
1937	Carmen Mastren	1958	Barney Kessel
1938	Benny Helier	1959	Barney Kessel
1939	Charlie Christian	1960	Barney Kessel
1940	Charlie Christian	1961	Wes Montgomery
1941	Charlie Christian	1962	Wes Montgomery
1942	Eddie Condon	1963	Charlie Byrd
1943	Eddie Condon	1964	Jim Hall
1944	Allan Reuss	1965	Jim Hall
1945	Oscar Moore	1966	Wes Montgomery
1946	Oscar Moore	1967	Wes Montgomery
1947	Oscar Moore	1968	Kenny Burrell
1948	Oscar Moore	1969	Kenny Burrell
1949	Billy Bauer	1970	Kenny Burrell
1950	Billy Bauer	1971	Kenny Burrell
1951	Les Paul	1972	John McLaughlin
1952	Les Paul	1973	John McLaughlin
1953	Les Paul	1974	John McLaughlin
1954	Johnny Smith	1975	Joe Pass
1955	Johnny Smith	1976	George Benson
1956	Barney Kessel	1977	Joe Pass

'down beat' MAGAZINE CRITICS' POLL WINNERS 1953–75 — GUITAR

The Established Talent winners are listed first;
winners in the Talent Deserving Wider Recognition
section appear to the right.

1953	Barney Kessel	Johnny Smith
1954	Jimmy Raney	Tal Farlow
1955	Jimmy Raney	Howard Roberts
1956	Tal Farlow	Dick Garcia
1957	Tal Farlow	Kenny Burrell
1958	Freddie Green	Jim Hall
1959	Barney Kessel	Charlie Byrd
1960	Kenny Burrell	Wes Montgomery
1961	Wes Montgomery	Les Spann
1962	Wes Montgomery	Grant Green
1963	Jim Hall/Wes Montgomery	Joe Pass
1964	Jim Hall	Gabor Szabo/Attila Zoller
1965	Jim Hall	Bola Sete
1966	Wes Montgomery	Rene Thomas
1967	Wes Montgomery	George Benson
1968	Kenny Burrell	Larry Coryell
1969	Kenny Burrell	Pat Martino
1970	Kenny Burrell	Sonny Sharrock
1971	Kenny Burrell	Dennis Budimir
1972	Kenny Burrell	Tiny Grimes/Pat Martino
1973	Kenny Burrell	George Benson/Attila Zoller
1974	Jim Hall	Ralph Towner
1975	Joe Pass	John Abercrombie
1976	Jim Hall	John Abercrombie
1977	Jim Hall	Derek Bailey

'down beat' MAGAZINE READERS' POLL RESULTS FOR GUITAR SINCE 1936 AND CRITIC'S POLL RESULTS FOR GUITAR SINCE 1953.

Reprinted with the permission of 'down beat'.

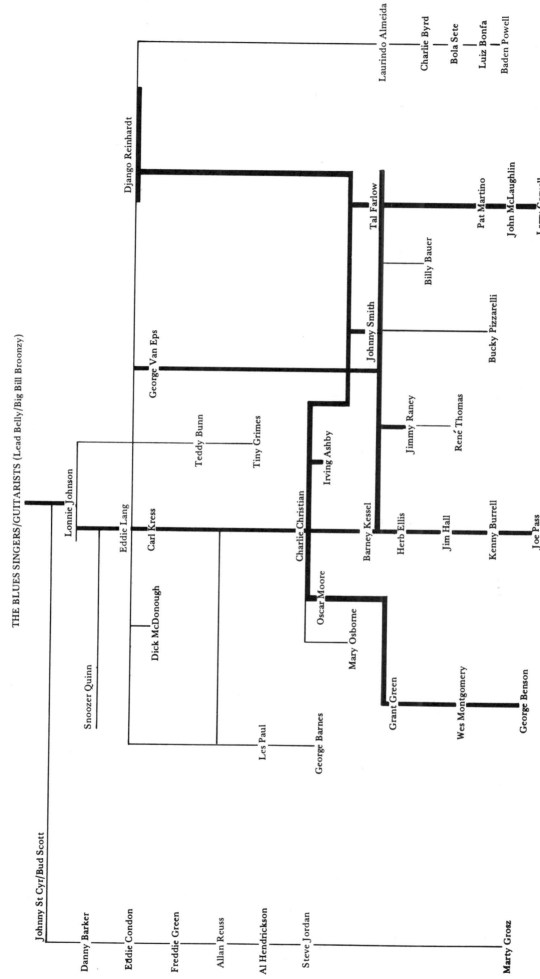

THE BLUES SINGERS/GUITARISTS (Lead Belly/Big Bill Broonzy)

1895

1978

Johnny St Cyr/Bud Scott

Danny Barker

Eddie Condon

Freddie Green

Allan Reuss

Al Hendrickson

Steve Jordan

Marty Grosz

Lonnie Johnson

Snoozer Quinn

Eddie Lang

Carl Kress

Dick McDonough

Les Paul

George Barnes

Django Reinhardt

George Van Eps

Teddy Bunn

Tiny Grimes

Charlie Christian

Irving Ashby

Oscar Moore

Mary Osborne

Grant Green

Wes Montgomery

George Benson

Barney Kessel

Herb Ellis

Jim Hall

Kenny Burrell

Joe Pass

Johnny Smith

Jimmy Raney

René Thomas

Bucky Pizzarelli

Billy Bauer

Tal Farlow

Pat Martino

John McLaughlin

Larry Coryell

Laurindo Almeida

Charlie Byrd

Bola Sete

Luiz Bonfa

Baden Powell

A Family Tree of the Jazz Guitar showing the main influences of the styles of the Jazz Guitar Greats from 1895—1978

24

THE JAZZ GUITAR

ITS PLAYERS

COURTESY ECM RECORDS

John Abercrombie

JOHN ABERCROMBIE

Born—Portchester, New York, U.S.A.

16th December 1944

John Abercrombie has proved to be one of the most influential jazz guitarists of the seventies. He has been closely associated with musicians such as Billy Cobham, Gato Barbieri, Jack De Johnette and also most recently with fellow guitarist Ralph Towner.

John first became interested in music and the guitar during his school years in Greenwich, Connecticut. Originally influenced by popular artists such as Bill Haley and the late Elvis Presley, John decided to take up the guitar and during the late fifties he was already playing in various rock bands at high school. It was at this time he heard his first jazz guitar records and the playing of Barney Kessel, Tal Farlow, Jimmy Raney, and Johnny Smith in particular, caused a deep impression on the young musician. The result being his decision to enter the Berklee College of Music from 1962—1966 in order to study his chosen instrument and music in depth. He was fortunate to be able to study under teachers such as Jack Peterson and Herb Pomeroy. The most important factor of his stay at Berklee was not just the general musical environment of this excellent institution but that John learnt how to bring the best out of himself musically.

After leaving Berklee John spent eight years in Boston gaining experience with various groups. His first job found him playing 1967—8 with organist Johnny 'Hammond' Smith. He claims that at this time the guitar style of Jim Hall greatly impressed him. After Boston John left for New York and played for a short while with drummer Chico Hamilton's group. After a brief return to Boston he joined Hamilton in 1971 to play at the Montreux Jazz Festival in Switzerland. He was given the opportunity to write for the group on a regular basis and this no doubt helped broaden his musical ability.

Like many of the younger jazz players John Abercrombie has been influenced by 'Rock' music and his style over the last few years has developed into one of the most tasteful and fluent of the ever growing band of Jazz/Rock musicians in the U.S.A. today.

SELECTED RECORDS

'Sorcery' with Jack De Johnette	Prestige	P10081
'Timeless'	ECM Records	ECM 1047
'Gateway'	ECM Records	ECM 1061
'Saragossa Sea' with Ralph Towner	ECM Records	ECM 1080

SELECTED READING

'Six String Stylistic Summit'	Chuck Berg—'Downbeat' 26th February 1976
'New Jazz Guitar Wizard'	John Stix—'Guitar Player' February 1976
'Abercrombie—Un Enfant du Rock'	'Jazz Magazine', March 1976
'John Abercrombie'	Lance Bosman—'Guitar', November 1977

Oscar Aleman with Frank 'Big Boy' Goudie circa 1935—Inset Oscar Aleman 1978.

COURTESY CHARLES DELAUNAY/OSCAR ALEMAN

OSCAR ALEMAN

Born—in the Chaco of Argentina

1905

Little is known today of the brilliant guitarist who earned a very high and well-deserved reputation in Europe from 1928–39. It is interesting to note that Leonard Feather, the leading American jazz critic, wrote recently of his high regard of Aleman. There is no doubt on listening today to some of the recordings made during the late thirties in Paris that he was a jazz guitarist of considerable talent.

Oscar Aleman's first musical instrument was the Brazilian ukulele, the Cavaquinho, after which he took up the guitar. At the age of 12 he was already a star and he was signed by a group called the Moreira Sextet. With this group he went to Brazil and it was there that he heard his first jazz record. In 1925 Aleman and the guitarist Gaston Bueno formed a duo called 'Los Lubos' and they worked in and around Buenos Aires. Though times were not easy the guitarists were given the opportunity for a tour of Spain backing the dancer Harry Fleming. At the end of this tour both Bueno and Aleman decided to stay on in Spain working in a Belga orchestra.

In 1932 the duo decided to split up. Josephine Baker who was at that time the number one cabaret artiste in Paris had heard of the exceptional musical talent of Oscar Aleman and offered him the guitar seat in her accompanying band at the Cafe de Paris. Through this break Oscar's ability became more widely known and he worked and recorded with violinist Svend Asmussen. At one time he replaced Django Reinhardt in Freddy Taylor's orchestra. It is obvious from listening to their records that both these great guitarists had some influence on each other. Aleman also made several records with Danny Polo under the supervision of Leonard Feather.

In 1941, presumably because of World War II, Aleman returned to Buenos Aires. For eighteen years Oscar Aleman had devoted his career to the jazz guitar but as time went on popular demand had swung towards Latin American rhythms. He did return to Europe but only for a short while. A further sign of the respect that Aleman had amongst leading jazzmen was the request of the late Duke Ellington on a visit to Buenos Aires in September 1968, to the U.S. Ambassador in Argentine, to find out where Aleman lived as he wished to meet this great guitarist in person. Today Oscar Aleman lives modestly in a flat in Buenos Aires where he devotes his life to teaching and playing the guitar.

SELECTED RECORDS

'The Guitar of Oscar Aleman'	The Old Masters	TOM31
'Oscar Aleman'	Redondell	110508

SELECTED READING

'Jazz Solography'—Vol. 4	Jan Evensmo

Oscar Aleman with the Freddy Taylor Orchestra, Paris, 1935.

COURTESY CHARLES E. H. SMITH

Laurindo Almeida

COURTESY CONCORD RECORDS/PHOTO PHIL LINDSAY

LAURINDO ALMEIDA

Born—San Paolo, Brazil

2nd September 1917

Laurindo Almeida is one of the most historic figures in the evolution of the jazz guitar, not so much from his fine technical ability on the instrument but from his overall musical talent and original concepts. Several years before the Bossa Nova movement swept the world it was he who introduced the idea of combining American jazz music with the traditional rhythms and melodies of his native Brazil.

Almeida received his early musical tuition from his mother who was a concert pianist. She had hoped that he too would become a pianist but Laurindo fell in love with the guitar owned by his sister Maria. In a short time it was evident to all around him that he was on the way to being a master guitarist.

Laurindo signed on as guitarist on the Brazilian liner *Cuyaba* in 1936. During the voyage to Europe he was able to absorb a wide variety of music including his first exposure to jazz. In particular on a visit to Paris he heard the 'Hot Club of France' starring Django Reinhardt.

On his return to Brazil Almeida settled in Rio and he took on the post of staff guitarist/arranger with Radio Mayrink Veiga. By 1944 Laurindo had reached the heights of his profession in Brazil and in 1947 he moved to the U.S.A. Here he worked in films and as a classical soloist with violinist Elizabeth Waldo.

His avid interest in jazz soon obtained him the guitar seat in the great Stan Kenton orchestra which was to become a legend over the whole world for its innovations in jazz music. His most outstanding recordings with Kenton were his solo work in Pete Rugolo's 'Lament' and his own 'Amazonia'. In 1950 Laurindo left the Kenton orchestra to lead a more diverse musical career.

During 1953—4 he joined forces with saxophonist Bud Shank and with addition of bass and drums recorded three brilliant records entitled 'Brazilliance'. These records were the forerunners of bossa nova, mixing Brazilian rhythms with American jazz. Almeida's impeccable taste in composing, arranging and playing shines through on all these records. He also started and continued to make many solo albums of both classical and popular music. In 1963—64 he toured the world as a featured soloist with the Modern Jazz Quartet. This association had begun as a project for the Monterey Festival in 1963. In recent years he has once more gained great popularity with his L.A. Four which features the saxophone of Bud Shank plus the bass of Ray Brown and drums of Shelly Manne. This group is a direct continuation of the concept of Laurindo's Brazilliance group established in the early sixties.

Laurindo is today one of the most popular and sought after guitarist/composers in Hollywood where he lives with his wife Deltra Eamon, the Canadian soprano, whom he married in 1971. He has won 10 'Grammy Awards' and as well as performing on the guitar he has a long list of film scores to his name (including amongst others 'Viva Zapata', 'The Godfather', 'A Star is Born'). He also has written many valuable music books, including an excellent tutor, which are of great value to the repertoire of the guitar.

SELECTED RECORDS

'Brazilliance 1'	World Pacific	WP1259
'Brazilliance 2'	World Pacific	WP1412
'Brazilliance 3'	World Pacific	WP1419
'Broadway Solo Guitar'	Capitol	ST2063
'Suenos'	Capitol	T2345
'Guitar from Ipanema'	Capitol	ST2187
'With the M.J.Q.'	Philips	BL7652
'Duo with Ray Brown'	Century City	CCR80102
'With Sammy Davis Jnr'	Reprise	RS6236
'With Stan Getz'	Verve	ST2419
'L.A. Four Vol 1'	Concord	CJ8

'L.A. Four Vol 2'	Concord	CJ18
'Latin Guitar'	Dobre	DR1000
'Virtuoso Guitar'	Crystal clear	CCS8001
'Guitar Player' Collection	MCA	MCA2—6002
'L.A. Four Pavane'	East Wind	EW10003

SELECTED MUSIC

Guitar Method	Criterion Music Corp.
'Guitariana' Seven Solos	Carlvi Music Co.
'Bossa Guitarra' Six Solos	Criterion Music Corp.
'Contemporary Moods'	Robbins Music Corp.
'Guitar Tutor'	Gwyn Publishing Co.
'Popular Brazilian Music'	Gwyn Publishing Co.

SELECTED READING

'Laurindo Almeida spans two worlds'	John Tynan—'Downbeat', July 24th 1958
'Laurindo Almeida'	Ivor Mairants—'Guitar', July 1974

Irving Ashby with the Nat King Cole Trio.

COURTESY MELODY MAKER

IRVING ASHBY

Born—Somerville, Massachusetts, U.S.A.

29th December 1920

Irving Ashby

Irving Ashby was born into a musical family, his mother was a pianist and his brother played the tenor guitar on which Irving first taught himself the rudiments of guitar playing. For a time he became interested in guitar construction and for a short period he worked as an assistant in the workshops of the Boston guitar maker, Stromberg.

In 1938 Irving was gigging in various dance groups and also planning to enter Boston University to major in Art and Writing, but he received an offer to join the new Lionel Hampton band. He decided this offer was too good to turn down. Although the standard of his music sight reading was not too good, Ashby used his excellent ear to get through the many written arrangements in the exciting Hampton band which included many of the world's top jazzmen at that time.

His featured solo with the band was his arrangement of 'Prelude in C Sharp Minor' by Rachmaninoff. He had received a scholarship on the basis of this solo several years earlier when he was at the New England Conservatory of Music. His guitar style at this time was greatly influenced by Charlie

Christian whom he had befriended.

During the war years Irving Ashby spent his service in the Army Band. After the end of the war in 1946 Nat King Cole offered Irving the guitar seat in his famous trio. This had recently been vacated by Oscar Moore and was at that time a prize spot for a guitarist to fill. This he was to do most admirably for four-and-a-half years.

As 'King Cole' became more and more commercial Ashby felt musically stifled and quit the trio only to become the first guitarist with the then newly formed Oscar Peterson trio. In 1952 he toured as Peterson's guitarist with Norman Granz's Jazz at the Philharmonic and this was probably the peak of his jazz career.

Although not an innovator on his chosen instrument Irving Ashby is a fine player and his talents have really been underestimated by guitarists and the jazz world as a whole. Today he lives in Perris, California, teaching the guitar and occasionally recording but spends much of his time sign painting and drawing architectural plans.

SELECTED RECORDS

'J.A.T.P. Concert'	Verve	2610 024
'California Guitar'	Famous Door	HL102
'Guitar Player Collection'	MCA	MCA 2—6002
'Memoirs'	Accent	ACS 5091

SELECTED MUSIC

'Guitar Work Book'	Trebla Publishing Co.

SELECTED READING

'Irving Ashby—Playing with the Greats'	Harvey Siders—'Guitar Player', September 1974

ELEK BACSIK

Born—Budapest, Hungary

22nd May 1926

Elek Bacsik

Elek Bacsik, a Hungarian gypsy, started his musical career studying the violin at the Budapest Conservatoire. In 1945 he fell in love with the guitar and from that time on devoted his musical studies entirely to it. Within four years he felt he had reached a standard good enough to play professionally.

Having served three years in the army, he joined the Hazy Osterwald band in 1949 in Switzerland and this engaged him in a long tour throughout Europe. He ended up in Paris in 1959, and played regularly in the renowned 'Mars Club' with pianist Art Simmons and bassist Michael Gaudry. This engagement lasted for two years. Until 1966 Elek played with many visiting U.S. jazzmen including trumpeter Dizzy Gillespie with whom he recorded, and befriended.

In 1962, he recorded in Paris an excellent session entitled 'The Eclectic Elek Bacsik', which fully displays the Hungarian's virtuosity and inventive mind. This recording remains today as one of the best European jazz guitar records of the period.

He decided to move to the U.S.A. in 1966 and has spent much of his time in Las Vegas doing commercial guitar work, involving himself little in jazz. In 1974 the promoter Bob Thiele encouraged him to come out of the obscurity of Las Vegas and he is now once more devoting some of his time to jazz. It can only be hoped that the very fine guitar work of Elek Bacsik will once more be brought into the limelight that it deserves.

SELECTED RECORDS

'The Eclectic Elek Bacsik'	Philips	680—221
'Dizzy on the French Riviera'	Philips	600—048

Derek Bailey

COURTESY GUITAR MAGAZINE/PHOTO DENNIS AUSTIN

DEREK BAILEY

Born—Sheffield, England

29th January 1932

Derek Bailey is today regarded as one of the pioneers of free jazz. He has a traditional background of music in that his grandfather was a professional pianist/banjoist and his uncle a professional guitarist. Derek himself started his professional career as a band guitarist working in theatres and popular night spots like London's 'Talk of the Town'.

Bailey found that after 10 years of playing in the field of popular music he was not getting any musical satisfaction. So in 1963 he was to become involved in jazz. He found himself fascinated by the sounds of free music and gradually he became one of the first generation of British free improvisors.

In 1963 Derek formed a trio with Gavin Bryars and drummer Tony Oxley. They played regularly at a Sheffield pub called 'The Grapes'. The group developed a small but loyal following. All three musicians decided to further their musical careers in jazz by moving to London in 1966. Since then Bailey has never looked back, making many records of his very individual free jazz music, solo, and also with a variety of other free jazz musicians for both English and German companies. He has the distinction of winning the 1977 'Downbeat' critics' poll for the jazz guitarist deserving wider recognition, but he has, as yet, not played in the U.S.A.

The sound of Derek Bailey's free jazz is hard to explain to jazz lovers who have not heard it, but in an article in 'Impetus' magazine Kenneth Ansell gives a clear description as follows:

'He has evolved a unique vocabulary for the electric guitar which he employs in his solo and ensemble work. Generally preferring a brittle, sparse sound his performances are always provocative, and often embody a kind of wry humour that will creep up on the listener almost unnoticed. He sits, concentrating his energies on his playing and that of those around him, producing a sustained flow of invention. He will use dry chords, aggressive torn notes or, through a combination of wah-wah and volume foot pedals, sounds that seem to materialise from the air and slowly disappear again. To describe his complete battery of resources from which he builds his music would be impossible, but suffice to say that he has extended the guitar vocabulary almost beyond recognition.'

To many, Bailey's music is controversial, many jazz listeners do not accept it as jazz music, yet there is no doubt that after ten years in this field of music Derek Bailey has an ever increasing audience for both his concerts and records and it will be interesting to see if he has a lasting effect on the evolution of the jazz guitar.

SELECTED RECORDS

'Derek Bailey Solo'	Incus	2
'Improvisation'	Cramps	CRSLP 6202
'Guitar Solos'	Virgin/Caroline	C1518
'Improvisations for Cello and Guitar'	ECM Records	ECM 1013
'The London Concert'	Incus	16
'Drops'	Ictus	003

SELECTED READING

'Derek Bailey'	Peter Riley, 'Guitar', July 1974
'Derek Bailey'	Kenneth Ansell, 'Impetus' 6 1977
'Improvisation its Nature and Practice in Music'	Derek Bailey, Latimer Press 1978
'Derek Bailey'	Barry McRae—'Jazz Journal' March 1978
'Derek Bailey'	Dennis Constant—'Jazz Magazine', March 1974
'Derek Bailey'	John Dalton—'Guitar', May 1978

Mickey Baker

COURTESY MELODY MAKER/PHOTO ALAN JOHNSON

MICKEY BAKER

Born—McHOUSTON BAKER Louisville, Kentucky, U.S.A.

15th October 1925

Mickey Baker's reputation amongst many guitarists is mainly as an author of various guitar books and tutors. But he has as well always been a working guitarist mainly in the Rhythm and Blues field. Today he is still musically active but based in Paris with his wife Sylvia.

As a boy Mickey lived in an orphanage and it was in the marching band of this orphanage that he first developed an interest in music. At the age of 16 Mickey ran away from the orphanage and ended up in New York paying his way as a labourer. By the time he was 19 having listened to many leading jazz artists, including Charlie Parker and Dizzy Gillespie, he had decided that he wanted to be a jazz musician.

The trumpet was his first choice but the finance needed to purchase a trumpet was too high so he decided to buy a guitar. A few teachers plus a few years' concentrated study gave Mickey Baker the ability in 1949 to head his own jazz group. But financially it was not successful and he decided to move to the West coast. Here the reception to his progressive style of jazz music was even less successful. Whilst trying to earn the money needed to get back to New York Baker heard the blues guitarist Pee Wee Creighton. He liked what he heard and saw that Pee Wee was earning a good living. The result was that he altered his style and returned to New York as a blues guitarist.

His judgement proved correct and Mickey Baker— blues guitarist found himself in great demand for the Atlantic, Savoy and King labels, mainly as a backing artist for stars such as Ray Charles, Big Joe Turner and The Drifters.

During the mid-fifties Baker felt he could improve his financial status by emulating the chart topping duo—guitar wizard Les Paul and singer Mary Ford. He joined forces with an ex-student of his called Sylvia and in 1957 they had a smash hit with a song called 'Love is Strange'. Their popularity was to last right through to 1961. With this success behind them Mickey and Sylvia were able to establish their own publishing and recording companies as well as their own night club. Mickey Baker had been working on his tutors and music albums since the early fifties and now was able to use his publishing company to get world-wide distribution.

Despite his success as a blues and popular guitarist Baker felt that he still wished to play more of his first love, the jazz guitar. He therefore decided to move with Sylvia to Europe where he hoped he could develop a more satisfactory musical life.

He bought a home in Paris and established a permanent French residence there. Since that time he has prospered writing, arranging, leading various groups and has to a great extent fulfilled his desire to continue playing his own distinctive style of jazz/blues guitar.

SELECTED RECORDS

'The Wildest Guitar of Mickey Baker'	Atlantic	8035
'Jazz Guitar Solos'—Mickey Baker	Kicking Mule Records	SNKF 127
'The Blues and Me'—Mickey Baker	Black and Blue	33 507

SELECTED PUBLICATIONS

'Analysis of the Blues'	Baker Publishing Co.
'Jazz Book 1'	Lewis Music Publishing Co.
'Jazz Book 2'	Lewis Music Publishing Co.
'Guitar Method 1—3'	Lewis Music Publishing Co.

SELECTED READING

'Mickey Baker'	Stefan Grossman—'Guitar Player' January 1976

DAVE BARBOUR

Born— DAVID MICHAEL BARBOUR
New York City, U.S.A. 28th May 1912

Died—Malibu, California, U.S.A.
11th December 1965

Dave Barbour

COURTESY JAZZ JOURNAL/PHOTO RAY WHITTEN

Dave Barbour started his career on the banjo but in common with many other banjoists at the time he changed to guitar and soon was featured with various small groups such as Wingy Manone in 1934 and Red Norvo's band 1935—6. In the late thirties Barbour, who was recognized as one of the most able jazz guitarists of the time, was regularly featured with top jazz artists such as Bunny Berigan, Teddy Wilson, Mildred Bailey and Louis Armstrong. He also worked in the big bands of Artie Shaw and Benny Goodman.

It was during his stay with the Goodman orchestra that Barbour met and married the superb jazz vocalist Peggy Lee. For some time he worked with her and together they wrote several hit songs including 'Manana' and 'It's a Good Day'. Their marriage broke up after nine years in 1952 and this also marked the end of his career as a jazz guitarist and as a full time working musician. In the last thirteen years of his life he was almost totally retired from music with exception of some record dates with singer Jeri Southern, and Nellie Lutcher.

Barbour appeared as an actor in several films during the fifties in various parts and in one entitled 'The Secret Fury' he actually appeared as a jazz guitarist.

SELECTED RECORDS

'Mildred Bailey'	Brunswick	LA8692
'Benny Goodman Orchestra'	CBS	88130
'B.B.B. & Co.'	Swingsville	2032

DANNY BARKER

Born—DANIEL BARKER, New Orleans, Louisiana, U.S.A.

13th January 1909

Danny Barker with Blue Lu Barker.

A nephew of drummer Paul Barbarin, Danny Barker's first instrument was the clarinet. His uncle then taught him the drums but Danny finally chose the ukulele and later the banjo, and guitar.

In the late nineteen twenties, he was featured with Lee Collin's ragtime band. He decided to move to New York in 1930 and for the next few years played guitar with many big jazz names including Albert Nicholas, Lucky Millinder and James P. Johnson. In 1938 he joined Benny Carter's big band and then from 1939 to 1949 he was with Cab Calloway. He had married the singer Blue Lu Barker and in 1946 he formed a backing group for her. Through the late nineteen forties and fifties Danny freelanced with most of the top traditional jazzmen including Bunk Johnson, Paul Barbarin and Albert Nicholas and in fact he was once more playing the banjo rather than the guitar.

Barker had played on both American coasts but in the late nineteen fifties he decided to settle in New York only to return home to New Orleans in 1965. Here he became assistant to the curator of the New Orleans Jazz Museum. Danny has remained in New Orleans since then spending his time playing, lecturing on jazz, and in 1969 he was a Grand Marshal for the New Orleans Jazz Festival. He continues in this position and still sometimes freelances with various groups in New Orleans, as well as lecturing on traditional jazz.

SELECTED RECORDS		
'Bunk Johnson Band'	Nola	LP 3
'Sidney Bechet Album'	Saga	Pan 6900

SELECTED READING	
'Bourbon Street Black'	Barker & Buerkle—Oxford University Press 1973

EVERETT BARKSDALE

Born—Detroit, Michigan, U.S.A.

28th April 1910

Everett Barksdale

Everett Barksdale's earliest professional experience was with the Erskine Tate band in Chicago. Following this he gained valuable experience playing with violinist Eddie South from 1932 for a period of almost ten years. During the nineteen forties he was featured with many leading jazz players including alto-saxophonist Benny Carter and also in radio work for the C.B.S. network.

His most prominent place in jazz probably came in 1949 when he joined the Art Tatum trio. Here he played some admirable guitar work with this incredible jazz giant of the piano for a period of almost seven years. In 1956 he took a break to become musical director for the vocal group 'The Inkspots' but rejoined Art Tatum's trio until the pianist's death on 4th November 1956.

He is currently a staff musician for the A.B.C. network in New York City and also is much in demand as backing musician on recording sessions supporting a variety of artists including Lena Horne, Sammy Davis Jnr., Dinah Washington and Sarah Vaughan.

SUGGESTED RECORD
'Art Tatum Trio—Live'   Jazz Anthology   30—JA 5138

Everett Barksdale with the Eddie South Orchestra.

Historic Jam Session—Red Norvo, George Benson, Benny Goodman, Teddy Wilson and Milt Hinton 1975.

COURTESY CRESCENDO/PHOTO DENNIS MATTHEWS

George Barnes

GEORGE BARNES

Born—Chicago Heights, Chicago, Illinois, U.S.A.
17th July 1921

Died—Concord, California, U.S.A.
5th September 1977

George Barnes came from a family of musicians. He was taught by his father, a guitarist, at the age of nine. Brought up in Chicago, a city that had become a centre of jazz development, Barnes claims that his main influences were clarinetist Jimmy Noone, in whose band he was playing at the age of 16, and also Benny Goodman and Louis Armstrong.

As a young boy he was associated with the great blues guitarist Lonnie Johnson who must have influenced him and he also listened to many records of Django Reinhardt. At the age of 14 Barnes had his own quartet and at the age of 17 he was already on the NBC staff in Chicago as guitarist, conductor, and arranger—a remarkable achievement. He held this position for five years until 1942 when he was drafted into the army. During the seven years up to 1942 George Barnes was often featured in recording sessions with many legendary Folk/Blues artists such as Big Bill Broonzy, Washboard Sam, and Blind John Davis.

On leaving the army after the war George returned to a life which was one of the busiest in jazz history. In 1951 he moved from Chicago to New York where his exceptional musical ability won him a contract with Decca Records as guitarist, composer and arranger. Because of his multiple talents he has also been much in demand over the years as a backing artist for many top line singers including Frank Sinatra and Bing Crosby.

He made many historic jazz recordings with various quartets and quintets but his greatest contribution to jazz guitar history were his unique guitar duos with Carl Kress (and then Bucky Pizzarelli after the death of Kress) and his recent quintet records led jointly with cornetist Ruby Braff.

Always a great individualist George Barnes had a very distinctive sound partly due to his personally designed cello/arch top guitar without the usual 'F' holes. This was made especially for him by the Guild Guitar Co., to his own design. In 1975 he moved to Concord, California, where he spent his time both playing at jazz clubs and teaching until his death after a heart attack in September 1977.

SELECTED RECORDS

'George Barnes Octet'	Hindsight	HSR—106
'Something Tender' with Carl Kress	United Artists	UAJ 14033
'Town Hall Concert' with Carl Kress	United Artists	UAS 6335
'Braff/Barnes Quartet'	Chiaroscuro	CR 121
'Braff/Barnes Quartet' play Gershwin	Concord	CJ 5
'Braff/Barnes salute Rodgers & Hart'	Concord	CJ 7
'Guitars—Pure and Honest'	A & R Records	7100—077
'The Guitar Album'	CBS	CBS 67275
'Barnes/Venuti Live'	Concord	CJ 30
'Blues Going Up'	Concord	CJ 43

SELECTED READING

'George Barnes'	Ivor Mairants, 'B.M.G.' December 1966
'George Barnes'	Bob Yelin, 'Guitar Player', February 1975
'George Barnes'	Ivor Mairants, 'Guitar', June 1975

SELECTED MUSIC

'George Barnes Electric Guitar Method'	Wm. J. Smith Music Co.	
'10 Duets for Two Guitars with Carl Kress'	Music Minus One	MM04011

BILLY BAUER

Born— WILLIAM HENRY BAUER New York City, U.S.A.

14th November 1915

Billy Bauer with Tony Aless (piano), Arnold Fishkin (bass).

COURTESY JAZZ JOURNAL

Originally a banjo player Billy Bauer turned to the guitar in the thirties and joined the Jerry Wald Orchestra. In the next few years he was to play with various bands including Carl Hoff, Dick Stabile and Abe Lyman. He reached particular prominence when he filled the guitar seat with the Woody Herman band in 1944.

After the Herman band disbanded in 1946, Bauer freelanced around New York with star musicians such as Benny Goodman and Chubby Jackson. It was at this time that he first met pianist Lenny Tristano and the fruits of this association were to prove to be Billy Bauer's most important contribu-

tion to the development of the jazz guitar. He ably matched the 'cool', 'free' style of Tristano and also that of alto-saxophonist Lee Konitz. Together they made some historic recordings. These records added new ideas and dimensions to jazz as it was then known and so have proved to be a milestone in jazz history.

Since that time Billy has left the limelight and really has gone into relative obscurity. He appeared in a Long Island club with his own group from 1961—3 and worked for a period as a staff guitarist with 'Ice Capades'. Much of his time since then has been devoted to teaching and his own publishing company.

SELECTED RECORDS

'Billy Bauer'—Plectrist	Norgran	1082
'Cross Currents' with Tristano	Capitol	M 11060
'Jazz Renaissance Quintet'	Mercury	MH 20605
Lee Konitz—Ezzthetic	Prestige	7827

SELECTED READING

'Remember Billy Bauer'	Ray Gogarty—'Guitar Player', April 1972
'Billy Bauer'	Ivor Mairants—'Guitar', April 1975

BILLY BEAN

Born—WILLIAM FREDERICK BEAN
Philadelphia, Pennsylvania, U.S.A.

26th December 1933

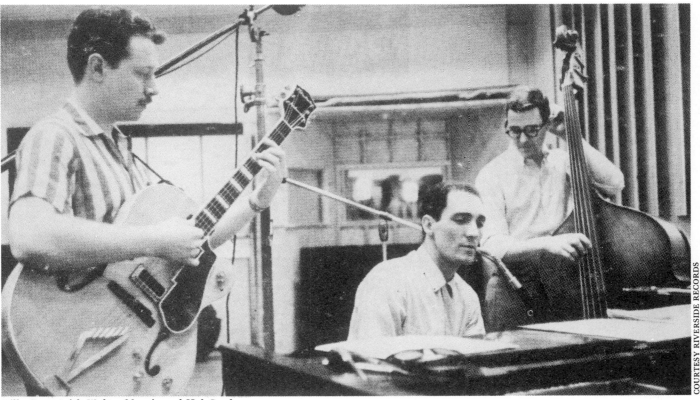

Billy Bean with Walter Morris and Hal Gaylor

Born into a musical family, his father was a guitarist and mother a pianist, Billy had the right environment for the serious study of his chosen instrument. After gaining a lot of experience with various bands in and around Philadelphia, he joined Charlie Ventura in 1956. Following in the footsteps of many of his fellow musicians he moved to California in 1958 and freelanced with various groups around the Los Angeles area. These groups included top jazz artists such as Buddy Collette, Paul Horn, Calvin Jackson, Bud Shank and Buddy de Franco.

Although a very able and inventive guitarist he has never as yet reached the forefront as a jazz guitar player despite some beautiful duo recordings with guitarist John Pisano on the Decca label.

SELECTED RECORDS

'The Trio'—Billy Bean	Riverside	ST380
'Take Your Pick'	Decca	9212
'Making It'	Decca/Brunswick	LAT 8272
'Fred Katz—Folk Songs'	Warner Bros.	1277

George Benson

COURTESY WARNER BROS.

GEORGE BENSON

Born—Pittsburgh, Pennysylvania, U.S.A.

22nd March 1943

In 1976 George Benson was voted by several popular and jazz polls as the world's number one jazz guitarist. During that year world-wide sales of his record 'Breezin' passed the 2,000,000 mark. Although the bulk of the sales were to a non-jazz audience purchasing the record for Benson's fine vocal ability and 'in' guitar sound, there is no doubt that he opened the ears of many young listeners to his fine jazz guitar playing. As a result Benson has created an interest for them to listen to other jazz guitarists.

Benson's stepfather, Thomas Collier, was a Charlie Christian fan and he taught George to play the ukulele at an early age. By the time he was eight George was already doing nightclub work with his stepfather, singing, dancing and also playing the ukulele.

In 1954 he began to study the guitar, borrowing guitars at friends' houses and then playing an electric guitar made for him by his father. By the time he was 17 he was already leading his own Rock and Roll group. Listening to records of various jazz artists including those of Hank Garland, Grant Green, Charlie Parker and in particular the late Wes Montgomery, George was encouraged to turn his musical talent towards jazz.

In 1962 Jack McDuff, on the recommendation of Don Gardner, hired George and this association lasted for three years giving the young guitarist valuable playing experience with top jazz artists.

After the outstanding popular success of Wes Montgomery's guitar sound, George Benson, whose guitar playing at that time so resembled Montgomery's, was an obvious choice for Creed Taylor, the producer of Montgomery's records, to repeat Montgomery's success after the great guitarist's death in 1968.

Creed Taylor's choice was to prove right, but the popular success he had hoped for Benson did not actually happen until 1976 when Benson's Warner Brother's record 'Breezin' even surpassed the record sales that Wes Montgomery had ever achieved.

A talented singer, Benson's guitar style now often veers towards Soul, and Rhythm and Blues music but he is still a very fine swinging jazz guitarist who can produce wonderful single note improvisations on the guitar. Although his popular success may mean that his full jazz potential may now never be heard, he does have the real ability to play fine jazz guitar in the future, and hopefully may do so.

SELECTED RECORDS

'New Boss Guitar'	Prestige	7310
'Benson/McDuff' (2 lp's)	Prestige	P 24072
'Its Uptown'	CBS	CBS 62817
'George Benson's Cookbook'	CBS	CBS 62971
'Shape of Things to come'	A & M Records	SP3014
'The other side of Abbey Road'	A & M Records	SP3028
'White Rabbit'	Creed Taylor	CTI 6015
'Breezin''	Warner Bros.	K56199
'In Flight'	Warner Bros.	K56327
'Weekend in L.A.' (2 lp's)	Warner Bros.	K66074

SELECTED READING

'Guitar in the Ascendancy—George Benson'	Stanley Dance, 'Downbeat', 29th June 1967
'The Essence of George Benson'	Herb Nolan, 'Downbeat', 7th June 1973
'George Benson'	Robert Yelin, 'Guitar Player', January 1974
'George Benson—In Conversation'	George Clinton, 'Guitar', May 1974
'Octave Soloing'	Michael Spector, 'Guitar Player', August 1976
'George Benson—Breezin' along with a Bullet'	Charles Mitchell, 'Downbeat', 9th September 1976

SKEETER BEST

Born– Kinston, North Carolina, U.S.A.

20th November 1914

Skeeter Best received his first musical education from his mother who was a piano teacher. His first professional work was with a local band led by Abe Dunn in the early thirties.

In 1940 he joined the Earl Hines orchestra, previous to which he had worked in Philadelphia with a band led by Slim Marshall. After leaving the U.S. Navy in 1945 he was featured in various jazz groups playing to servicemen in Japan and Korea.

Included in these groups was one led by the legendary bassist Oscar Pettiford in 1951–2.

Since that time Skeeter has freelanced around the New York City area playing and recording with many top jazzmen including saxophonist Paul Quinichette, and drummer Kenny Clarke. Although Skeeter Best has never reached great prominence he is known amongst jazz musicians as a respected and able guitarist.

SELECTED RECORDS

'Sir Charles Thompson Trio'	Vanguard	PPT 12020
'Modern Jazz Sextet' (with Dizzy Gillespie)	Columbia	33CX 10048
'Blow Your Horn' Paul Quinichette Sextet	Brunswick	LAT 8099
'Quinichette/Gonsalvez'	Communication	CO 300
'The Chase and the Steeplechase'	MCA	510127

Al Avola guitarist with the Artie Shaw Band for many years.

COURTESY MELODY MAKER

ED BICKERT

Born—EDWARD ISAAC BICKERT
Hochfield, Manitoba, Canada

29th November 1932

Ed Bickert

Ed Bickert grew up in Vernon, British Columbia, and started playing the guitar at the age of eight. Both his parents were musicians playing in a country music band and Ed sometimes played with them at dances.

By the time he was 20 Bickert moved to Toronto where he worked for a local radio station as well as doing studio and jazz work. He was often featured with the Moe Koffman Quintet and Rob McConnell's Boss Brass.

For many years Ed has played at the well-known Bourbon Street jazz club in Toronto, accom-panying top U.S. jazz musicians including Red Norvo, Chet Baker, Paul Desmond, Frank Rosolino and Milt Jackson. He also often plays there with his own trio, although he does spend much of his professional time in the television and recording studios in Toronto.

In the last few years Bickert has recorded several albums with other jazz artists and two with his own group. In 1976 he played at the Monterey Jazz Festival with Paul Desmond, and is now regarded as one of Canada's leading guitarists both in the commercial and jazz fields of music.

SELECTED RECORDS

'I like to recognize the Tune'	United Artists	UALA 747G
'Ed Bickert'	P.M. Records	PMR 010

SELECTED READING

'Ed Bickert'—Profile	Mark Miller—'Downbeat', 20th May 1976

LUIZ BONFA

Born— LUIZ FLORIANO BONFA Rio de Janeiro, Brazil

17th October 1922

Luiz Bonfa

Luiz Bonfa's greatest impression on the jazz world, has been his compositions, in particular his musical score for the film 'Black Orpheus' (Manha de Carnival, Samba de Orfeu etc.), but he is also a very fine guitarist in the traditional Brazilian style, as can be heard on his many records.

He began to play the guitar at the age of 12 under the tutelage of his father who was also a guitarist. He continued his studies under Isaias Savio a master classical guitarist, and Bonfa attained very high standards in the classical field. He decided, after giving several concert recitals on the classic guitar, to give his attention to the field of popular music.

In 1946 he started his professional career in Brazil that made him one of the top performers both on the radio and stage. At one time he sang and played the guitar in a group called the 'Quitandinha Singers'. In 1958 he decided to move to the U.S.A. where his arrival was luckily to coincide with the Bossa Nova boom. The singer Mary Martin was greatly impressed by Luiz' guitar artistry and he accompanied her for several concerts in 1958—9. During this time he became exposed to jazz for the first time. He then made several very successful recordings with tenor saxophonist Stan Getz and also some with his wife, singer Maria Toledo.

Today, Luiz Bonfa continues to lead a highly successful career as a guitar player, singer, and composer on the west coast of America. His multi-talents being much in demand for films, television and the recording industry.

SELECTED RECORDS

'Le Roi de la Bossa Nova'	Fontana	680—228
'Bossa Nova'	Verve	SVLP 9209
'Braziliana'	Philips	BL 7703
'The Brazilian Scene'	Philips	SBL 7727
'Jazz Samba/Stan Getz'	Verve	SVLP 9013
'Jacaranda'	Ranwood	R8112
'The New Face of Bonfa'	RCA	LSP 4376

BOULOU

Born— BOULOU FERRÉ Paris, France

24th April 1951

Boulou

COURTESY CHARLES DELAUNAY/PHOTO ETIENNE DOBIECKI

Boulou Ferré was born into a family of musicians. His father Matelot Ferré, and uncles Sarane and Barreau Ferré are all prominent French guitarists. Boulou was taught from the age of eight by his father, who was at one time a guitarist in the Quintet du Hot Club de France accompanying Django Reinhardt. By the time Boulou was nine he had already given his first concert.

Regarded by many as a child prodigy, Boulou studied both the classical and plectrum guitars, and his musical style was influenced both by Segovia and jazz masters Charlie Parker and Dizzy Gillespie. His greatest jazz guitar influences were Django Reinhardt, Wes Montgomery and Tal Farlow. At the age of twelve-and-a-half Boulou made his first recording under the direction of Alain Goraguer on the Barclay label. This record and another one made a little later on the Barclay label under the direction of Jean Boucherty are proof of the amazing talent Boulou had at such a young age.

Over the years Boulou has based himself in Paris and has worked with a variety of jazz artists including Dexter Gordon, Stephane Grapelli, Gordon Beck, and T. Bone Walker. He has appeared many times on French television and was featured on classical guitar at Vence Festival in 1976. He played at the Antibes Jazz Festival in 1965 with Bernard Lubas and Gilbert Rovere, and also starred in several concerts at Olympia in Paris. Duke Ellington was greatly impressed by Boulou's playing and told the young guitarist that he was continuing the great tradition set by Django Reinhardt. Today still only twenty-six-years old Boulou could well reach the top of the jazz guitar scene in the next few years.

SELECTED RECORDS

'Boulou'	Barclay	80311
'Boulou and the Paris All Stars'	Barclay	CBLP 2083

Lenny Breau

COURTESY GUITAR PLAYER/PHOTO BOB HUNKA

LENNY BREAU

Born– **LEONARD BREAU** Auburn, Maine, U.S.A.

5th August 1941

Lenny Breau was discovered by top country guitarist Chet Atkins in Winnipeg, Canada. Headlined to be the jazz guitar find of the sixties Breau has been until recently in virtual self-retirement basically due to ill health. Certainly from the evidence of his two recordings on the RCA label, he is a most versatile and individual stylist on the guitar.

Lenny started playing the guitar at the age of seven and by the time he was 12 he was able to join his parents, country and western singers Lone Pine and Betty Coty, professionally.

His first interest in jazz was when he was 17 when he listened to and was influenced by most of the leading guitar innovators of the fifties such as Barney Kessel, Tal Farlow and Johnny Smith. But his particular style of guitar playing which he has

developed can be closely aligned to the finger style of Chet Atkins and the piano approach of Bill Evans. When Chet Atkins heard Breau in Winnipeg he immediately recognized the young player's unique ability and signed him to make a record for the RCA label.

After the success of this first record Breau spent some time in Los Angeles where he played at Drummer Shelley Manne's jazz club 'The Manne Hole', amongst several other dates. In the late sixties he returned to Toronto and then Winnipeg from 1973–5. He is currently living in Killaloe, Ontario, Canada, very rarely giving public performances although with the persuasion of Chet Atkins and others, he has been spending some time in Nashville teaching and playing occasional club dates.

SELECTED RECORDS

'Guitar Sounds from Lenny Breau'	RCA	LSP4076
'Velvet Touch of Lenny Breau'	RCA	LSP4199

SELECTED READING

'Lenny Breau–Atkins Style Jazz' Martin K. Webb–'Guitar Player', September 1974

Big Bill Broonzy

COURTESY JAZZ JOURNAL

'BIG BILL BROONZY'

Born—WILLIAM LEE CONLEY   Scott, Mississippi, U.S.A.
26th June 1893

Died—Chicago, Illinois, U.S.A.
14th January 1958

Big Bill Broonzy the legendary singer/guitarist whose music is the very essence of the blues and of early jazz music, was raised in Arkansas. His mother had been born into slavery, and as a young man Bill made his living as a farm worker.

Exposed to many of the early blues guitarists, Broonzy developed a moving, bluesy style on the guitar which accompanied his voice and others.

In 1920 he moved to Chicago where he worked as a labourer. He became a member of the local black community and as a result he associated with legendary blues singers and instrumentalists including Tampa Red, Memphis Minnie, Memphis Slim and Leroy Carr. He also took guitar lessons from Papa Charlie Jackson. His talents were obvious and soon he was hired by Paramount as a guitar accompanist for various blues singers in 1926.

By the late 1930's he had already established himself as a top blues vocalist in his own right and was recording regularly. In 1938—9 he was a featured artist in John Hammond's 'Spiritual to Swing' concerts.

During the war Broonzy dropped out of the limelight and worked as a janitor at the Iowa State College. Fortunately he was still able to maintain a musical career in Chicago and as a result his whereabouts were known to jazz lovers throughout the world.

In 1951—2 because of popular demand he toured Europe and the United Kingdom. These tours were so successful that they not only ensured that his greatness was fully recognized but created a demand for further concert tours in 1955 and 1957. A lung operation in late 1957 brought Bill's singing career to an end and he died of cancer the following year.

The greatness of Big Bill Broonzy as a blues singer is undisputed. But it is perhaps not generally realized that his 'bluesy' swinging guitar playing was without doubt one of the finest and most influential of the many primitive blues guitar styles, probably affecting many of the solo jazz guitarists who have heard his music.

SELECTED RECORDS

'Big Bill Broonzy'	Queen Disc	Q—023
'Big Bill Broonzy'	MSI Disc	30 JA 5127
'Big Bill Live'	Storyville	670 143
'Remembering Big Bill'	Mercury	60905
'Big Bill Broonzy'	Black and Blue	33—012
'Big Bill Sings Country Blues'	XTRA	1093

SELECTED READING

'Big Bill Broonzy'	A Biography as told to Yannick Bruynoghe Cassell & Co. 1955
"Big Bill"	'This is Jazz' p. 89—96 Yannick Bruynoghe Newnes 1960
'Big Bill's Last Session'	Studs Terkel—'Guitar Player', April 1973

DENNIS BUDIMIR

Born— DENNIS MATTHEW BUDIMIR
Los Angeles, California, U.S.A.

20th June 1938

Dennis Budimir

At the age of 19 Dennis Budimir's reputation on the guitar had already earned him the guitar seat in the Harry James band. Following his stay with this band he returned to his native California where his first jazz work was with drummer Chico Hamilton, after which he began a successful association with saxophonist Eric Dolphy.

The experience gained with these groups helped Budimir develop his own individual jazz style which on analysis is obviously more orientated to the style of saxophonists Sonny Rollins and John Coltrane than other guitarists. Following his work with the Dolphy quintet Dennis Budimir served two years in the Los Angeles studios mainly backing singer Peggy Lee. This gave him valuable experience and also the training to develop a fine reputation as a commercial guitarist. He maintained his interest in jazz when he replaced Billy Bean for a while in the Bud Shank quartet.

In 1963 Dennis left Peggy Lee but joined pianist Bobby Troup for a tour of Japan. Since then he has worked as a highly respected studio musician in the Los Angeles area with a wide variety of artists including, Quincy Jones, Lalo Schiffrin, Don Ellis, Julie London and Marty Paich.

Much admired by other West Coast guitarists Budimir won the 'Downbeat' critics' poll in 1971, but his fine guitar work is little known to the general jazz listener for his own records as a leader on the Revelation label are not easily found.

SELECTED RECORDS

'Alone Together'	Revelation Rev 1
'A Second Coming'	Revelation Rev 4
'Sprung Free'	Revelation Rev 8
'Session with Albert'	Revelation Rev 14

TEDDY BUNN

Born— THEODORE LEROY BUNN
Freeport, Long Island, New York, U.S.A.

1909

Teddy Bunn with Al Norris (centre) and Ulysees Livingstone (right).

COURTESY JAZZ JOURNAL/PHOTO PETER TANNER

Teddy Bunn was a mainstay of the world famous 1930's vocal/instrumental group, 'The Spirits of Rhythm'. His unique guitar style greatly influenced guitarists of the period and although never really featured as a guitar soloist in his own right, his great inventiveness, swing and ability on the guitar have never been in doubt amongst the bulk of jazz lovers.

Bunn was a self-taught player but had an excellent ear which helped him quickly master his chosen instrument. In the mid-nineteen twenties he accompanied various blues singers and in 1928 he

was featured with the 'Washboard Serenaders'. Few people realized that for 18 months he temporarily replaced Freddie Guy as guitarist with the Duke Ellington orchestra. In the nineteen thirties he came to prominence when he replaced Buddy Blanton in the 'Spirits of Rhythm' who at that time were regularly featured at the jazz night-spot in New York City, the 'Onyx Club' in 52nd Street.

In 1937 Bunn worked for a time with the original John Kirby band but in 1939 rejoined the 'Spirits of Rhythm'. In 1944 this great guitarist led his own group called the 'Waves of Rhythm' and in the following years he fronted his own small bands in Sacramento and Los Angeles.

Since the war this historically very important guitarist has freelanced mainly on the West Coast of the U.S.A. with traditional jazz artists such as Johnny Dodds, Jimmie Noone, and Mezz Mezzrow. In the mid-nineteen fifties he worked with Edgar Hayes, Jack McVea and Louis Jordan, and in the late fifties was actually featured for a time with a Rock and Roll band. In 1970 he worked in a night club in Honolulu but since then his health has been suffering and this has forced him to cease working. Today he lives at his home in San Fernando, California.

SELECTED RECORDS

'The Spirits of Rhythm'	Caete	LP—1
'Johnny Dodds—Blues Galore'	MCA	510—106
'Sidney Bechet Jazz Classics Vol 1'	Blue Note	1201
'50 Years of Jazz Guitar'	Columbia	33566
'Kings of the Guitar'	Beppo	14800
'Ladnier/Mezzrow/Bechet'	RCA	FXM 1—7132

SELECTED READING

'Teddy Bunn on Record'	R. G. Craik—'Jazz Journal' June 1971
'Teddy Bunn on Record Part 2'	Peter Tanner—'Jazz Journal', July 1971
'Teddy Bunn'	Ivor Mairants—'Guitar', May 1973
'Teddy Bunn Today'	Peter Tanner—'Jazz Journal' October 1976

COURTESY MELODY MAKER

Jimmy Lunceford rhythm section with Al Norris on guitar.

COURTESY MELODY MAKER

Top British Guitarists of 1937 at Abbey Road Studios. Left to Right: Harry Pike, Don Stutely (bass), Sam Gelsley, Albert Harris, Ivor Mairants.

Kenny Burrell

COURTESY CONCORD RECORDS/PHOTO PHIL LINDSAY

KENNY BURRELL

Born—KENNETH EARL BURRELL
Detroit, Michigan, U.S.A.

31st July 1931

Kenny Burrell's music career began in his home town of Detroit. Under the tutelage of his elder brother Billy, Burrell started playing the guitar at the age of 12. Kenny originally wanted to play the saxophone, but the high cost of the saxophone influenced him to choose the guitar instead. The young guitarist was fortunate in that he not only had a solid musical background at home, his father was a banjoist, his mother a pianist, and both brothers guitarists. At school many of his friends were also musicians including pianist Tommy Flanagan and bassist Calvin Jackson. His musical advisor at Miller High School was Louis Cabrara and this was to prove most useful and influential in shaping Kenny's musical career. It is of interest that other ex-pupils of Miller High School include vibist Milt Jackson and saxophonists Yusef Lateef and Pepper Adams.

Kenny's early influences on the guitar were Charlie Christian and Oscar Moore and by 1948 he already was well known locally. He played in many groups in the Detroit area including a spell with trumpeter Dizzy Gillespie at the Club Juana. In 1955 he led his own group but left to fill the guitar seat in the Oscar Peterson Trio recently vacated by Herb Ellis. He stayed with Peterson for only six months but the break from Detroit made Kenny decide to settle in New York where he has lived until the present time. He was first hired by pianist Hampton Hawes, and then he worked with saxophonist Frank Foster and trumpeter Thad Jones.

Over the years Kenny has successfully led his own groups in New York jazz clubs, making many recordings over the years which are very popular amongst jazz lovers throughout the world. He did spend some time playing with Broadway theatre orchestras (including 'Bye Bye Birdie' and 'How to Succeed in Business'), and even tried his luck as a vocalist on a Columbia recording but this did not meet with success.

Kenny now also regularly plays in jazz clubs and at jazz festivals both in the U.S.A. and Europe. In 1957 he played with Benny Goodman. From 1952—3 he studied the classical guitar and he now occasionally uses this technique on the finger style instrument as part of his performance. Determined to educate himself musically to the full he studied music at Wayne University where in 1955 he received his Bachelor of Music degree, and this too considerably contributes to the overall guitar sound and music of Kenny Burrell.

Kenny's love and involvement with the guitar has always been great as was seen by his interest in promoting the instrument at a jazz club called 'The Guitar' in New York, which is now unfortunately closed. This was originally organized by fellow Detroiter—Fred Hayes who had studied at Wayne University with Burrell. In 1973 he became involved in studio work in the Los Angeles area as well as continuing concerts, clubwork and seminars. In recent years he has continued to win many jazz polls and it is said the late Duke Ellington let it be known that Kenny was his favourite guitarist.

SELECTED RECORDS

'Introducing Kenny Burrell'	Blue Note	1523
'Kenny Burrell'	Blue Note	1543
'Blue Lights) Vol. 1'	Blue Note	1596
'Blue Lights—Vol. 2'	Blue Note	1597
'Kenny Burrell Quintet at the Five Spot'	Blue Note	4021
'Two Guitars'—Burrell/Raney	Prestige	7119
'Weaver of Dreams' (Vocal)	Columbia	1703
'Kenny Burrell'	Prestige	7088
'Kenny Burrell/John Coltrane' (2 lp's)	Prestige	P24059
'The Best of Kenny Burrell'	Prestige	7448
'All day long, All night long' (2 lp's)	Prestige	PR24025
'Asphalt Canyon Suite'	Verve	V6—8773

'Blues—The Common Ground'	Verve	SVLP—9217
'Guitar Forms'	Verve	VLP—9099
'Night Song'	Verve	VLP—9246
'Cool Cooking'	Checker	6467—310
'Ode to 52nd Street'	Cadet	LPS—798
'Both Feet on the Ground'	Fantasy	9427
'Ellington in Forever'	Fantasy	F7—9005
'Up the Street'	Fantasy	9458
'Tin Tin Deo'	Concord	CJ 45

SELECTED PUBLICATIONS

'Jazz Guitar Solos'	Chas. Colin Music
'Jazz Guitar'	Elliot Music Co.

SELECTED READING

'Kenny Burrell'	Ira Gitler, 'Downbeat', 1st August 1963
'Kenny Burrell—In his own Right'	Dan Morganstern, 'Downbeat', 14th July 1966
'Kenny Burrell'	Ivor Mairants, 'B.M.G.' October 1969
'Man with a Mission'	Lewis K. McMillan Jnr., 'Downbeat', 10th June 1971
'Kenny Burrell'	'Guitar Player', March 1971

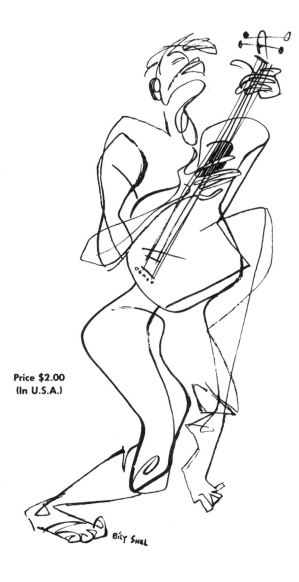

JAZZ GUITAR
KENNY BURRELL

Price $2.00
(In U.S.A.)

Recorded JAZZ GUITAR
Solos Authentically Transcribed

Contents

MIDNITE BLUES
36—23—36
BLUES IS AWFUL MEAN
CHITLINS CON CARNE
WAVY GRAVY
COME ON BABY
BLUES AFTER ALL
SUGAR HILL
LYRESTO
SOUL LAMENT
SATURDAY NITE BLUES
HOOCHI COO
MULE
BLUES FOR LIZ
CLEO'S ASP
TRAVELIN
KENNY' SOUND
BLUES FOR DEL

Chas. Colin

publishers of new sounds in modern music
315 West 53rd Street New York 19, N.Y.

BILLY BUTLER

Born—WILLIAM BUTLER   Philadelphia, Pennsylvania, U.S.A.

1924

Billy Butler

Billy Butler began playing the guitar professionally in 1940 with a group called 'The Three Tones'. He had started on the guitar at the age of 13 and was virtually self-taught. Originally inspired by acoustic guitarists Eddie Lang and George Van Eps, it was the electric guitar sounds of Charlie Christian, George Barnes and Oscar Moore that were to prove the major influences on Billy's jazz style.

In 1943 Butler joined the Army and he was put into a military band as a drummer. After his discharge he returned home to Philadelphia where he was featured with a vocal quartet called 'The Harlem-Aires'. He spent three years with a band called 'Daisy May and the Hepcats' and in 1952 he formed his own group. It was in 1955 that success came to Butler, now regarded as a top blues guitarist, when he joined organist Bill Dogget. They made a record called 'Honky Tonk' which sold a million copies. Following on this popular success Butler stayed with Doggett for a further eight years.

In the last few years Billy has established himself as a top studio artist in New York and is often heard in bands accompanying Broadway shows. Yet he is still involved in making a few records which have established him as a jazz player. On one recently released record he is featured with guitarist Al Casey.

SELECTED RECORDS

'That Healin Feelin'	Prestige	7601
'This is Billy Butler'	Prestige	7622
'Guitar Soul'	Prestige	7734
'Guitar Odyssey' with Al Casey	Jazz Oddysey	012
'Don't be that Way'	Black and Blue	33—014

SELECTED READING

'Billy Butler Honky Tonk'	'Guitar Player' March 1975

COURTESY CONCORD RECORDS/PHOTO PHIL LINDSAY

Charlie Byrd

CHARLIE BYRD

Born — CHARLES L. BYRD
Chuckatuck, Nr. Suffolk, Virginia, U.S.A.

16th September 1925

Charlie Byrd

COURTESY JAZZ JOURNAL

Charlie Byrd started to play the guitar at the age of nine, studying with his father who played several stringed instruments, the mandolin being his main instrument. Charlie's first professional work was to be with a dance band at the Virginia Polytechnic Institute. Later he toured Europe with an Army show band under the direction of Marty Faloon. It was whilst he was in Paris that he was able to hear and play with the legendary Django Reinhardt. After leaving the Army Byrd remained in the New York City area for four years from 1946 playing jazz with many groups which included various well-known jazz artists such as Joe Marsala.

Although a plectrum guitarist at that time Charlie began to take a serious interest in classical music and the classical guitar. Bill Harris, the classical guitarist from Washington DC told him of the fine teaching ability of Sophocles Papas a noted guitarist/educator who was a resident of Washington. In 1950 Byrd decided to devote his time to studying the classical guitar in Washington with Papas, and at the same time, theory and harmony with musicologist Thomas Simmons. Since then Washington DC has been the home and

base for Charlie Byrd. One of the highlights of Byrd's career was when he joined Andre Segovia's master class in Siena, Italy. He also spent a short time on tour as guitarist with the Woody Herman band.

But it was to be his newly found interest in the classic guitar which in fact was to bring Charlie Byrd's name to the forefront of jazz guitar lovers. He had at one time decided to give up jazz, but after some experimentation he founded his historic jazz trio comprising of himself on classic guitar, Keeter Betts—double bass and Berstell Knox—drums. They played nightly sessions to packed houses at his own Washington jazz club—'The Showboat Lounge'. The bulk of the music at these sessions was jazz but Charlie would successfully intermingle several solo classical guitar pieces.

This new trio and Charlie's original style of finger style guitar jazz caused a real stir in the jazz world. In 1961 the U.S.A. State Department sponsored a tour for the guitarist's trio to South America. It was during this tour that the idea occurred to Byrd of mixing jazz improvisation with the samba and other popular Brazilian rhythms. On his return home to the U.S.A. in 1962 he made the historic and best selling record with tenor saxophonist, Stan Getz, entitled 'Jazz/Samba'. Despite the fact that Bud Shank and Laurindo Almeida had produced similar records entitled 'Brazilliance' a few years earlier, Byrd's choice of music including compositions by top Brazilian writers, like Antonio Carlos Jobim and Joao Gilberto, brought an enormous commercial success for this recording. The combination of Getz's saxophone and Byrd's guitar probably was the real start of the fantastic Bossa Nova boom in the U.S.A. and eventually the rest of the world.

For some time after the success of 'Jazz/Samba', Byrd made many records which sold in large quantities, outselling 100 per cent jazz records by other top line guitarists. In 1965 he was chosen to play for President Johnson in the White House, and Byrd regularly won International Jazz Polls.

With the decline of Bossa Nova in recent years Byrd's popularity has waned somewhat but in the last year or so he has been touring the U.S.A. with the 'Great Guitars' a successful group which includes fellow guitarists Barney Kessel and Herb Ellis.

SELECTED RECORDS

'Solo Flight'	Riverside	9498
'Latin Impressions'	Riverside	9427
'Meditation'	Riverside	9436
'Mr. Guitar'	Riverside	9450
'Byrd's Word'	Riverside	9448
'Byrd in the Wind'	Riverside	9449
'Blues Sonata'	Riverside	9453
'Byrd at the Gate'	Riverside	9467
'Byrd Song'	Riverside	9481
'Once More' Charlie Byrd	Riverside	9454
'At the Village Vanguard'	Riverside	9452
'The Guitar Artistry of Charlie Byrd'	Riverside	9451
'Jazz Recital'—Charlie Byrd	Savoy	12099
'Jazz/Samba'	Verve	2317—006
'Travellin' Man'	Columbia	2435
'Stroke of Genius'	Columbia	30380
'Guitar/Guitar'	Columbia	9130
'Great Guitars' Vol. 1	Concord	CJ 4
'Great Guitars' Vol. 2	Concord	CJ 23
'Top Hat'	Fantasy	F9496

SELECTED MUSIC

'Charlie Byrd's Melodic Guitar Method'	Hollis Music Inc.
'Jazz 'n' Samba Album'	Hollis Music Inc.
'Charlie Byrds/Bossa Nova'	Peter Maurice Co.
'Three Classic Guitar Blues'	Columbia Music Co.
'Great Movie Themes for Guitar'	Edward B. Marks Co.

SELECTED READING

'Chuckatuck's Gift to the Guitar—Charlie Byrd'	Tom Scanlan, 'Downbeat', 21st July 1960

AL CASEY

Born— **ALBERT ALOYSIUS CASEY** Louisville, Kentucky, U.S.A.

15th September 1915

Al Casey and his Trio.

Like Teddy Bunn and Lonnie Johnson, Al Casey's ability and influence on the jazz guitar have been very underrated in many jazz circles. A gifted player, Casey has a distinctive, punchy single-note style on the acoustic plectrum guitar which is complemented by his superb rhythmic chordal style playing.

Al's father was a professional drummer and other members of his family helped make up the famous spiritual group 'The Southernaires' which broadcast from Cincinatti in the early thirties. He first started his musical career on the violin which his mother taught him from the age of five but Al changed to the guitar in 1930 when he moved to New York City. He first came to prominence as a sideman in the legendary combo led by pianist/singer Fats Waller. He had been introduced to Waller when 'The Southernaires' had played with Waller on a radio show. The pianist showed real interest in Casey who was studying at the Martin Smith music school, and promised him a job when he finished high school. In late 1933 he graduated and as promised, at the age of 17, he joined Waller's band. He was with Fats Waller from 1934 to 1943 and the sound of his guitar was an integral part of both of Waller's small and large groups. He did have a break for one year from Waller in 1939—40 when he was the guitarist in the Teddy Wilson band. His time with Waller was to be the greatest influence on his style of jazz. Casey called the pianist 'his second father'.

After Fats Waller's death Casey led his own trio and also worked with several smaller groups, including that of Louis Armstrong, for five years. Jazz lost Casey in 1949 for a while to Rock and Roll when he joined the King Curtis band and then Curley Hamner's group. Casey changed to a solid electric guitar for this work.

Fortunately in recent years, Al has returned to jazz and his acoustic guitar, working and recording both in the U.S.A. and Europe. He has worked with top musicians like Bob Wilber, Milt Buckner and Jay McShann and it is hoped that he will now produce many more fine recordings.

SELECTED RECORDS

'Ain't Misbehavin' '—Fats Waller	RCA Victor	LPM 1246
'Buck Jumpin'	Prestige	2007
'Slamboree'	Black and Blue	33—049
'Jumpin' with Al'	Black and Blue	33—056
'Guitar Odyssey' with Billy Butler	Jazz Odyssey	012

SELECTED READING

'Al Casey—Back on the Scene'	Stanley Dance—'Downbeat', 19th July 1962

PHILIP CATHERINE

Born— London, England

27th October 1942

Philip Catherine with Larry Coryell (left).

Philip Catherine is one of the most respected of the young jazz/rock guitarists both as a player and composer. He was originally inspired by European guitarists Django Reinhardt and René Thomas, probably because his father was a Belgian and Philip lived his early years in Belgium. In the late nineteen fifties and sixties Philip played with various jazz groups in Belgium including those of Fats Sadi and Jack Sels. He was also featured on the Belgian Radio.

In the early seventies he was strongly influenced by the growing jazz/rock movement, in particular by guitarists John McClaughlin and Larry Coryell. From 1970—2 he worked with avant-garde violinist Jean Luc Ponty. After leaving Ponty he decided to go to the U.S.A. where he spent a year studying at the Berklee School of Music. In 1973 he formed his own jazz/rock group called 'Pork Pie' which he led together with saxophonist Charlie Mariano. He is currently touring and recording with guitarist Larry Coryell as a duo after they were billed together successfully at the 1976 Montreux Jazz Festival by the organizer, Claude Nobs.

SELECTED RECORDS

'Grapelli/Ponty'	Inner City	1005
'Guitars'—Philip Catherine	Atlantic	K50193
'Twin House' Duo with Larry Coryell	Atlantic	50342
'September Man'	Atlantic	48562

SELECTED READING

'Corryell/Catherine'	Terry Theise, 'Guitar', August 1977

PIERRE CAVALLI

Born — Zurich, Switzerland

12th July 1928

Pierre Cavalli

Encouraged by his parents, who were both keen on music, Pierre Cavalli originally studied the violin from the age of five. He changed to the guitar and after reaching professional standard on this instrument he settled in Paris in 1953 where he was much in demand as a freelance guitarist. He worked with top musicians and groups such as those of Quincy Jones and Michel Legrand. His fine musical ability was often featured in their many films, scores and commercial orchestral arrangements.

Currently he spends most of his time playing throughout Europe, both in the recording studios and as sideman with various top jazz artists including violinist Stephane Grapelli. He is little known outside of Europe although he did play for a short time in Las Vegas.

SELECTED RECORDS

'Strictly Guitar'	HMV	7EG 8817
'Stephane Grapelli Quintet'	Atlantic	1391

SELECTED MUSIC

'Strictly Guitar'—Guitar Solos	Lawrence Wright Music Co.

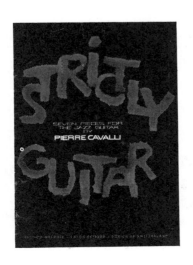

Charlie Christian

COURTESY MELODY MAKER

CHARLIE CHRISTIAN

Born– CHARLES CHRISTIAN Dallas, Texas, U.S.A.
1919 (Recent investigations suggests the year to be 1916)

Died—New York City, U.S.A. 2nd March 1942

Charlie Christian grew up in Oklahoma City where all four of his brothers were musicians, and his father was a singer/guitarist. Charlie started his musical career on the trumpet but due to a chest condition turned to the guitar at the age of 12, although he also had knowledge of the bass and the piano.

During the early 1930's he played in his brothers' band 'The Jolly Jugglers' but first drew real professional recognition and importance when he joined the Anna Mae Winburn Orchestra in 1937 and later with the Al Trent Sextet in 1938. Charlie had heard the basic efforts on the electric guitar by Eddie Durham and Floyd Smith in the mid-nineteen thirties and he decided to experiment with the amplified guitar himself.

His reputation on the electric guitar grew very quickly and jazz lovers came from far and wide to hear his new and original guitar style. His single note lines sounding so like a mellow tenor saxophone. During these years he was to develop many original ideas into his jazz improvisations. He used augmented and diminished chords in a way which in the not too distant future would be known as Be Bop. Though his jazz ideas were very individual he particularly loved the guitar style of Django Reinhardt. He would get a great kick out of playing Django's improvised choruses, note for note, on numbers like 'St. Louis Blues' and then carrying on to play his own improvisations.

In 1939 whilst playing with the Leslie Sheffield Band he was heard by the influential jazz promoter John Hammond who persuaded top band leader Benny Goodman to hear Christian play in Oklahoma City. Although originally reluctant to hear the young guitarist,it took only a few bars for the great clarinettist to recognise the guitarist's genius and special talent and Charlie was signed up on the spot.

In the two years that followed Charlie Christian became not only a profound influence on the Benny Goodman Big Band and Sextet but also on the history of jazz itself. After playing at night with Goodman, Charlie would play into the early hours of the morning at Mintons' club in Harlem.

Here he played for hours on end experimenting and playing, his exciting improvisations directly influencing the now legendary jazz artists Thelonious Monk, Dizzy Gillespie, Kenny Clarke, Charlie Parker and others. Some of these sessions were fortunately recorded for posterity by Jerry Newman for the Estoreric Label.

Unfortunately the late nights and Charlie's lust for living a full life did not help his generally poor health. He had suffered from tuberculosis most of his life and in the summer of 1942 he suffered a serious relapse. He entered Bellevue Hospital where he remained until his death on 2nd March 1942 in a Staten Island Sanitarium.

On the cover of a Philips record BBC 7172 (now deleted) there are some excellent notes on the importance of Charlie Christian by Al Avakian and Bob Prince. To give a clearer picture of the Christian's vital contribution to jazz I can do no better than quote from these.

'His improvisations sound simple and effortless but when analysed, prove complex and daring in their explorations of musical principles. These complexities were not contrived, but were the result of Christian's natural inventiveness and drive, bringing forth a new, mobile, swinging jazz that resulted in a basic influence on modern musicians.

'Charlie's greatest asset was his command of rhythm. He had a natural drive to swing at all costs, and this, coupled with his spontaneous explorations of rhythmic principles, led him to a flexibility of beat that was unique. This flexibility became a pre-requisite in all forms of jazz to follow.

'Charlie's basic beat was the modern, even four-four, but his solos are full of metric denials. They are remarkable illustrations of mobile swing.
'Christian had complete and easy control over rhythm and on the basis of this rhythmic freedom, he constructed his phrasing. A singular aspect of his phrasing is the unusual length of his melodic lines, consisting of even and clearly executed notes. His meter was delineated by the subtle accent of certain of these eight notes.

'Charlie Christian considered no interval "wrong".

In his eighth-note phrases, running up and down the basic chords, he extended the chords to include other intervals such as the ninth, flattened ninth, eleventh, augmented eleventh, thirteenth and flattened thirteenth. In addition, his partiality for the dinished seventh chord, and his superimposition of this chord over basic harmonic progressions, can be heard in any number of his solos.'

Charlie Christian's legacy to the advancement of jazz music as a whole is indisputable. His style of playing has directly influenced the major jazz guitar artists such as Barney Kessel, Jim Hall, Tal Farlow and Herb Ellis, and really there could be few jazz guitarists today that have not been affected by Christian in some way.

SELECTED RECORDS

'Charlie Christian with Benny Goodman'	Columbia	CBS 52538
'Solo Flight'	Columbia	CBS 67233
'Minton Sessions'	Estoreric	ES 548
'Charlie Christian—Live'	Jazz Archives	JA 23
'Charlie Christian/Lester Young-Together'	Jazz Archives	JA 6
'Kings of the Guitar'	Beppo	Bekos 148000
'Trumpet Battle at Mintons'	Xanadu	107

SELECTED MUSIC

'The Art of Jazz Guitar'	Regent Music Corporation
'Charlie Christian Bop Guitar'	Smith Tharp Publishing Co.
'The Swingiest Charlie Christian'	Charles Colin Music Co.
'Six Charlie Christian Solos—Upbeat'	'Downbeat', 20th July 1961
'A Charlie Christian Blues Solo'	'Downbeat' p. 36, 11th June 1970

SELECTED READING

'Charlie Christian'	Morgan & Horricks, 'Modern Jazz' p.30—42, Gollancz 1957
'Charlie Christian'	Bill Simon, 'The Jazz Makers' p. 316—331, Peter Davis
'Combo U.S.A.'	Rudi Blesh (Chapter—Flying Home) Chilton Book Co. 1971
'Jazz Solography' Vol. 4	Jan Evensmo
'On with Charlie Christian'	Ernest E. Dyson, 'Downbeat', 11th June 1970
'L'Ectrique et Eclectique Charlie Christian'	'Jazz Magazine', July 1970
'Charlie Christian 1939—41'	A Discography, John Callis, Middleton Publication 1977
'Meeting Charlie Christian'	Barney Kessel, 'Guitar Player', Feb./Mar. 1977

HOT JAZZ GUITAR SOLOS

BOOK NO. 1
SMITH - THARP PUBLISHING CO.
P. O. Box 3002   Pueblo, Colorado

FEATURING
Charlie Christian
JAZZ BOP GUITAR

Price - $2.00

THE ART OF THE JAZZ GUITAR
CHARLIE CHRISTIAN

Edited by
DAN FOX

Includes a biography of Charley Christian and complete analyses of his solos

Price $2.00

REGENT MUSIC CORPORATION
1619 BROADWAY · NEW YORK 19, N. Y.

JOHN COLLINS

Born— **JOHN ELBERT COLLINS** Montgomery, Alabama, U.S.A.

20th September 1913

John Collins with the Nat King Cole Trio.

John Collins originally studied music with his mother a well-known band leader called Georgia Graham. He toured with her band from 1932—5. In 1935 he joined pianist Art Tatum which he followed with a three year stint with trumpeter Roy Eldridge. From 1940—2 he worked in New York City with many top jazz men including Benny Carter, Fletcher Henderson, Lester Young and Dizzy Gillespie.

After a four year spell in the Army Collins joined bassist Slam Stewart from 1946—8 and then pianist Rolly Taylor from 1949—51. On the recommendation of Irving Ashby he then filled the guitar seat in the Nat King Cole trio in 1951 until the singers death in 1965. Always respected as a fine guitarist and mature soloist by fellow musicians, Collins was relegated to a background role for the 14 years he spent with Nat King Cole and his solo guitar work is today relatively unknown.

For six years until 1971 Collins toured with pianist Bobby Troup's Quartet and he was once more able to show some of his fine ability on the guitar. Since that time John has free-lanced around the Los Angeles area leading his own quartet and backing artists such as Sammy Davis Jnr, Frank Sinatra, and Nancy Wilson.

SELECTED RECORDS

'Esquire's All American Hot Jazz'	Vintage	LPV544
'Browns Bag'	Concord	CJ19
'Guitar Player'	MCA	MCA2—6002

COURTESY JAZZ JOURNAL

Eddie Condon with his band.

EDDIE CONDON

Born—ALBERT EDWIN CONDON
Goodland, Indiana, U.S.A. 16th November 1904

Died—New York City, U.S.A.
4th August 1973

No one will deny Eddie Condon's greatness in the history of jazz both as an organiser and leader of various jazz groups. The fact that he played the banjo and then the four string guitar is secondary, it gave him a legitimate reason for being on the bandstand with his group. As a guitarist Condon really made no influence on jazz music as he did not solo, his rhythm playing, although felt by his fellow artists in the group, was always very discreet.

Eddie Condon was brought up in Momence in Chicago Heights, Illinois. He was self-taught on the ukulele and banjo and from the age of 15 was already working professionally with various groups. As a musician based in Chicago in the nineteen twenties he was associated closely with other top jazzmen such as drummer Gene Krupa and saxophonist Bud Freeman. In 1927 he recorded with 'The Chicagoans' jointly led by Red McKenzie and himself. Recordings made by this group are today recognized as being the most authentic 'Original Chicago Style Jazz'.

In 1928 Condon moved to New York City and played with a band called the 'Mound City Blues Blowers' and also with trumpeter Red Nichols. For several years he was often included as a sideman with several historic bands including those of Bobby Hackett and Artie Shaw plus many small groups on the legendary 52nd Street.

It was in 1939 that he established himself as a promoter of jazz. He not only promoted concerts in New York City Town Hall but he was to open his own club in Greenwich Village in 1946.

The combination of his love for jazz and his organizing ability became well known and he became a popular personality in 1948 with his own television show. His passion and devotion for Dixieland music brought happiness and pleasure to both player and listener. He never pretended to be a guitar 'maestro', having made the early transition from banjo to four string guitar in the late twenties but his background guitar playing was an integral part of all his groups.

From 1954 through 1957 he toured the U.S.A. and the United Kingdom. In 1958 he moved his club to the upper east side of 56th Street and then later to 54th Street where it still remains today as a permanent tribute to this great jazz personality. Until his death in 1973 Eddie Condon was still actively engaged in concerts and club work, leading his band and promoting the special type of jazz that he loved.

SELECTED RECORDS

'Jazz as it should be Played'	Jazzology	J50
'Condon a la Carte'	Commodore	FL 30—010

SELECTED READING

'Jazz's Evelyn Waugh'	Don Cerulli—'Downbeat', December 1956
'Eddie Condon's Scrapbook of Jazz'	St. Martins Press 1973
'We called it Music'	H. Holt 1947
'Eddie Condon's Treasury of Jazz'	Dial Press 1956
'Reminiscences of Eddie Condon'	Dan Morganstern—'Downbeat', 11th February 1965
'Eddie Condon, Paul Smith Recalls'	Rod Davies, 'Guitar Player', November 1975

Larry Coryell

COURTESY VANGUARD RECORDS

LARRY CORYELL

Born—Galveston, Texas, U.S.A.

2nd April 1943

Regarded as one of the major jazz/rock guitarist-composers of the seventies, Larry Coryell is reputed to have started playing the ukulele at the age of 12 although he had previous musical experience on the piano.

In 1950 his family had moved from Texas to Richmond, Washington and there his musical taste developed initially at the age of fifteen, into Rock 'n' Roll. He had progressed teaching himself, graduating from the ukulele to a student guitar and then to an electric guitar. Originally inspired by artists like Chet Atkins and Chuck Berry, he started taking lessons from a teacher who introduced him to the jazz guitar sounds of Wes Montgomery, Tal Farlow and Barney Kessel.

Whilst studying at the University of Washington in Seattle he decided that his future lay in music, in particular jazz and the guitar. At first he gigged in and around Seattle but then moved to New York City he was further influenced by local jazz musicians including Charles Lloyd. His first major job was with drummer Chico Hamilton's Quintet but it was only when he joined Gary Burton in 1967 in the vibist's first quartet, that his ability became recognized world-wide. In 1968 Coryell left Burton determined to lead his own group and within a short time he was leading the now renowned 'Eleventh House'. Since that time he has continued to develop as an individual and influential soloist both with his own groups and with other bands. Recently he has been featured at Jazz Festivals and on record with another contemporary jazz guitarist Philip Catherine.

SELECTED RECORDS

'Barefoot Boy'	Flying Dutchman	10139
'The Essential Coryell'	Vanguard	VSD 75176
'Offering'	Vanguard	79319
'At the Village Gate'	Vanguard	VSD 6573
'The Restful Mind'	Vanguard	VSD 79353
'Spaces'	Vanguard	79345
'Twin House' with Philip Catherine	Atlantic	50342
'Aspects'	Arista	AL 4077
'Guitar Player'	MCA	MCA 2—6002

SELECTED READING

'Coryell—Le Nouveau Passeur'	'Jazz Magazine, December 1969
'Larry Coryell—Now'	George Hoefer, 'Downbeat', 29th June 1967
'Larry Coryell—Levelling Off'	Neil Terser, 'Downbeat', 26th February 1976
'Larry Coryell'	Fred Stuckey, 'Guitar Player', August 1970
'The Eleventh House'	Michael Brooks, 'Guitar Player', December 1974
'Larry Coryell'	Ralph Denzer, 'Guitar', April 1975
'Coryell/Catherine'	Terry Theise, 'Guitar', August 1977

SELECTED MUSIC

'Improvisations from Rock to Jazz'	Guitar Player Productions

BILL DE ARANGO

Born—WILLIAM DE ARANGO, Cleveland, Ohio, U.S.A.

20th September 1921

Bill De Arango with Ben Webster.

Bill De Arango started his professional musical career playing with various local groups in 1939–42. After leaving the Army in 1944 he moved to New York City where he was featured with tenor saxophonist Ben Webster for a short period on 52nd Street. For a time he led his own group with the star vibist Terry Gibbs in both New York and Chicago. Since 1954 Bill has been out of the limelight despite a reputation amongst jazz musicians as being a modern soloist of the first order.

He is currently living in his home town Cleveland where he has his own music store. He still plays jazz in several local clubs on an occasional basis at nights.

SELECTED RECORDS

'Bill De Arango'	Em Arcy	MG 26020
'Ben Webster Septet'	Vogue Coral	10021

SELECTED RECORDS

'Bill De Arango'	EM Arcy MG26020
'Ben Webster Septet'	Vogue Coral 10021

SELECTED READING

'Bill De Arango'	Mark Gardner, 'Jazz Journal', July 1971

Al Di Meola

COURTESY CBS RECORDS

AL DI MEOLA

Born—Jersey City, New Jersey, U.S.A.

22nd July 1954

Al Di Meola is regarded as one of the leaders of the young jazz/rock guitarists, coming to world-wide prominence as part of the famed 'Return to Forever' group in 1974.

Raised in Bergenfield, New Jersey, Al started on the drums at the age of five and the guitar at eight. By the time he was in his early teens he had already played with various school bands playing both steel and standard electric guitars. Country music had a great appeal at that time for the young guitarist but when he was sixteen he heard a record by Larry Coryell. Al was so impressed that he took every opportunity that he could to hear Larry 'live' in the New York clubs. He was fortunate to develop a friendship with Coryell which gained him valuable knowledge and contacts.

On leaving high school Di Meola went to the Berklee College of Music in Boston. He left Berklee

for a few months to play with the Barry Miles quintet, but returned to the college to study arranging and further his musical education.

Di Meola's growing reputation as a guitarist came to the ears of keyboard player Chick Corea and in 1974 he offered Al a job with the 'Return to Forever' without an audition after hearing some tapes made by the Barry Miles quintet featuring Al's playing. This was an amazing stroke of luck as Corea's group was Di Meola's favourite at that time.

Al made several best selling records with 'Return to Forever' earning himself in a short time a very big reputation he recently has made three records as a leader on both acoustic and electric guitars, which have proven to be very popular. There seems no doubt now that Al Di Meola will become one of the most influential of the jazz/rock guitarists of the seventies.

SELECTED RECORDS

'Return to Forever/forgotten Warrior'	Columbia	CBS 81221
'Land of the Midnight Sun'	Columbia	PC 34074
'Elegant Gypsy'	Columbia	PC 34461
'Casino'	Columbia	JC 35277

SELECTED READING

'Al Di Meola'	Jim Crockett, 'Guitar Player', October 1975
'Guitar Sound Forum'	Lee Underwood, 'Downbeat', 24th February 1977
'Al Di Meola'	Vic Trigger, 'Guitar Player', February 1978

JOE DIORIO

Born—JOSEPH LOUIS DIORIO
Waterbury, Connecticut, U.S.A.

6th August 1936

Joe Diorio

Diorio studied music and the guitar originally at the Berdice School of Music from 1949 to 1954. From that time he has developed his own unique style which has kept his guitar style much in demand since the early sixties. He has played with a wide variety of top jazz artists including Eddie Harris, Bennie Green, Stan Getz, Ira Sullivan, Freddie Hubbard and Stanley Turrentine.

Although originally working in the Chicago area he moved to Miami which has been his base ever since. There he has continued developing his jazz guitar style as well as working on local television shows and writing books for the guitar. In 1975 he also began studying drawing and painting in Miami.

His most important jazz work of recent has been his duo work with the late pianist Wally Cirillo, and also his solo guitar work on Spitball records.

SELECTED RECORDS

'Move On Over' with Sonny Stitt	Cadet	S730
'Rapport' with Wally Cirillo	Spitball	SB—1
'Solo Guitar'	Spitball	SB—2
'Soloduo'	Spitball	SB—3
'Straight Ahead' with Steve Bagby	Spitball	SB—5
'Peaceful Journey'	Spitball	SB—7

SELECTED READING

'Joe Diorio'—'A profile'	'Coda' June 1972
'Joe Diorio'	David D. Spitzer, 'Guitar Player', August 1976

SELECTED MUSIC

'Intervallic Designs'—Joe Diorio	REH Publications

Sacha Distel and his Trio playing on board an Air-France jet at 10,500 metres.

COURTESY JAZZ JOURNAL.

SACHA DISTEL

Born—Paris, France

29th January 1933

Now virtually known throughout the world as a top line popular singer, Sacha Distel in the late nineteen fifties was regarded by many as France and Europe's leading modern jazz guitarist.

Distel is the nephew of the continental band leader Ray Ventura. His father was a chemist and his mother a singer and pianist. As a result his first musical experience was on the piano but on the advice of a friend he took up the guitar at the age of 15. His first work was with various college groups but he gained national prominence by winning an amateur talent contest at the age of 18. From the age of 19 he was constantly featured and recording with top jazz artists such as Bernard Pfeiffer, Henri Salvador, Bobby Jaspar, Kenny Clarke and John Lewis. In 1954 and 1956 he won the magazine 'Jazz Hot's' poll and also their critic's prize in 1957. He won the International Jazz Club prize in 1957.

Whilst playing in Paris at clubs like the 'Club St. Germain' he gained a lot of press publicity from his association with film star Brigitte Bardot. Later, on a six month trip to the U.S.A. he befriended saxophonists Stan Getz and Gerry Mulligan. For two-and-a-half years he backed the famed French Chantreuse Juliette Greco and it was during this time he developed his own individual singing style. In 1958 Sacha made his first hit record as a vocalist. In recent years he has not played the guitar professionally but has devoted all his time to a highly successful career as a much-in-demand, popular singing star throughout the world.

SELECTED RECORDS

'Afternoon in Paris' with John Lewis	Oriole	MG 20036
'From Paris with Love' (vocal)	RCA Victor	LPM 2611
'Bobby Jaspar All Stars'	Em Arcy	36105

EDDIE DURAN

Born—EDWARD LORENZO DURAN
San Francisco, U.S.A.

6th September 1925

Eddie Duran began playing the guitar from the age of 12. Previous to this he had studied the piano. Both his brothers were musicians and after leaving the Navy after the Second World War he has played and lived in the San Francisco area. Amongst the many top jazzmen he has played with in that time are world famous artists such as Stan Getz, George Shearing, Charlie Parker, Flip Philips and Red Norvo.

Very highly rated by his fellow musicians, Eddie Duran is little known outside the San Francisco area except on a few recordings which are evidence of his very attractive and lucid jazz guitar playing.

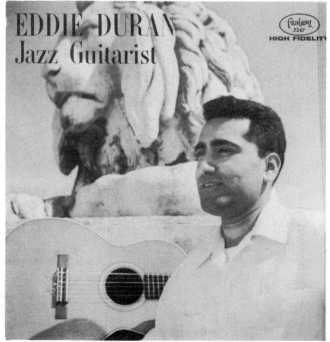

Eddie Duran

SELECTED RECORDS

'Eddie Duran'	Fantasy	3—247
'Vince Guaraldi Trio'	Fantasy	3—225
'Vince Guaraldi Trio'	Fantasy	3—257

Eddie Durham

COURTESY VALERIE WILMER

EDDIE DURHAM

Born—San Marcos, Texas, U.S.A.

19th August 1906

A prominent jazz musician of the nineteen thirties Eddie Durham is known mainly as a trombonist and composer, who also played the guitar. His importance to jazz guitar history is that he was the first jazzman to play an electrically amplified guitar and it was he who personally demonstrated it to Charlie Christian in 1937.

Though Eddie Durham's first instrument was the guitar, it was on the trombone that he gained his first professional experience. He played with circus bands during the early nineteen twenties, touring the Southern States of America. In 1926 he joined a 12 piece jazz group called 'The Dixie Ramblers'. He then was featured with groups led by Gene Coy and Walter Page, and in 1929 Eddie was part of Bennie Moten's Kansas City Band.

In the following years Durham was associated with many of the top names in jazz including Count Basie, Cab Calloway and Jimmy Lunceford. In fact whilst he was with Lunceford in 1935, Durham experimented with methods to amplify his guitar and with an aluminium resonator attached to his instrument he made the first recorded jazz solo on an 'amplified' guitar on a record called 'Hittin' the Bottle' with the Lunceford band.

Whilst he was with Count Basie, Eddie played in several small band sessions for jazz promoter John Hammond. In 1938 he made some recordings for Hammond with this group which was known as the 'Kansas City Six' and these included Durham's historic electrically amplified guitar solos. Already in 1937 Durham had met Charlie Christian in Oklahoma City and there he demonstrated his amplified guitar to the young man who would within a couple of years start a new era in jazz with his electric guitar. It was Durham who also introduced the electric guitar to Floyd Smith who in 1939 made the hit record 'Floyd's Guitar Blues' with the Andy Kirk band on an electric steel guitar.

Eddie Durham's greatest contribution to jazz has probably been his compositions and arrangements for bands such as Count Basie, Artie Shaw, Glenn Miller and Jimmy Lunceford in the nineteen thirties and forties. But there is no doubt that his experiments with amplifying the guitar had a great effect on the evolution of the jazz guitar. Since the end of the Second World War he has continued his career in the New York City area including a spell on both trombone and guitar with Buddy Tate in 1969. Of late most of his professional time has been spent on the trombone.

SELECTED RECORDS

'Jimmy Lunceford Harlem Shout 1933–6'		MCA 510 018
'Kansas City Six'	Ace of Hearts	ZAHC 176

SELECTED READING

'Eddie Durham'	George Hoeffer, 'Downbeat', 19th July 1962
'A La Naissance de la Guitare Electrique'	Valerie Wilmer—'Jazz Magazine' February 1976
'Eddie Durham'	Valerie Wilmer—'Coda' December 1977

COURTESY CONCORD RECORDS/PHOTO PHIL LINDSAY

Herb Ellis

HERB ELLIS

Born— MITCHELL HERBERT ELLIS
Farmersville, Near Dallas, Texas, U.S.A.

4th August 1921

Herb Ellis like many other leading American jazz guitarists (including Charlie Christian, Eddie Durham, Oscar Moore, and Lightin Hopkins) was born in the South Western part of the U.S.A. A bluesy and hill-billy flavour is one of the outstanding and distinctive features of Herb's playing and is most certainly due to the environment in which he was brought up.

The banjo was Herb's first stringed instrument, although it is claimed he played the harmonica at the age of four. The guitar soon followed the banjo and this was the instrument that Herb was playing when he entered the North Texas State College in 1941. Here he met and befriended many now well known jazz musicians including Jimmy Giuffre, Gene Roland and Harry Babasin. Herb joined Glen Gray's band after two years at college and in 1945 joined the Jimmy Dorsey big band for a period of three years.

Following this Herb formed his own instrumental/vocal trio called the 'Softwinds' which played together for five years. During this time Herb wrote several successful tunes such as 'Detour Ahead' and 'I Told You I Love You—Now Get Out'. But the real turning point in Herb's jazz career came when he took over Barney Kessel's seat in the Oscar Peterson Trio. There is no doubt that during his five year stay with Oscar, and his subsequent four years accompanying the renowned jazz singer Ella Fitzgerald all over the world, Herb developed his musical abilities to the full and became recognized world-wide as being amongst the elite of modern jazz guitarists. In fact, when Herb decided to leave the trio, Peterson decided to change the guitar seat in his trio to drums, after experiencing a short and unsuccessful period with Kenny Burrell on guitar. This decision was due mainly to the impossibility for Peterson to replace Herb at that time with any comparable guitarist, in particular one who could match his fantastic rhythmic abilities and outstanding solos at very up-tempo speeds.

Today Herb is settled in Hollywood and for a time was very active in the recording studios and on television. For many years he was a regular member of the Don Trenner Band which was featured on the famous 'Steve Allen Show' and was one of the most sought after musicians in the Hollywood Studios, featured with artists such as Della Reese and Joey Bishop. Fortunately he is now once again actively involved in jazz particularly with the Concord Festival and Recording Company in Los Angeles. He has made in recent times several excellent jazz records including some with fellow guitarists Joe Pass, Charlie Byrd and Barney Kessel and many other musicians including bassist Ray Brown and pianist Russ Tomkins.

SELECTED RECORDS

'Man with the Guitar'	Dot	25678
'Ellis in Wonderland'	Columbia	33LX 10066
'Nothing but the Blues'	Columbia	33LX 10139
'Herb Ellis meets Jimmy Giuffre'	Verve	CLP 1337
'Bossanova Time' with Laurindo Almeida	Epic	BA 17036
'The All Stars'	Epic	65890
'Guitar/Guitar' with Charlie Byrd	CBS	BPG 62552
'Thank you Charlie Christian'	Verve	MGV 8381
'Hello Herbie' with Oscar Peterson	MPS	BMP 20723—4
'Concord Festival' with Joe Pass	Concord	CJ 1
'Seven come Eleven' with Joe Pass	Concord	CJ 2
'Soft Shoe'	Concord	CJ 3
'Two for the Road' duo with Joe Pass	Pablo	2310—714
'Rhythm Willie' with Freddie Green	Concord	CJ 10
'Great Guitars' Vol. 1	Concord	CJ 14
'A Pair to Draw' with Russ Tomkins	Concord	CJ 17
'Great Guitars' Vol. 2	Concord	CJ 23
'Poor Butterfly'	Concord	CJ 34

SELECTED MUSIC
'Herb Ellis Jazz Guitar Style'   Mills Music Co.
'Jazz Duets' with Joe Pass   Gwyn Publishing Co.
'In Session' record and music (3001 St)   Guitar Player Productions

SELECTED READING
'Herb Ellis'   John Tynan—'Downbeat', 16th July 1964
'A Life in Jazz'   Daniel Sawyer—'Guitar Player', December 1972
Herb Ellis   Arnie Berle—'Guitar Player', April 1978
Herb Ellis   Mike Joyce—'Cadence' March 1978

Herb Ellis

COURTESY POLYTONE

BUS ETRI

Born— ANTHONY ETRI New York City, U.S.A.
1917

Died—Los Angeles, U.S.A. 21st August 1941

Bus Etri with the Charlie Barnet Orchestra.

Due to his early death Bus Etri is little known to jazz lovers today yet most of those who heard him play have no doubt that he would have become one of the greats of the jazz guitar.

Bus Etri's first real professional work was with the Hudson De Lange band in 1935, but he only came to prominence when he joined the Charlie Barnet band in 1938. His recordings with the band show him to be a swinging single note player and one of the band's best jazz soloists. But after being with the band for only three years Etri was tragically killed in a car accident near Los Angeles in 1941. The car was driven by vocalist Lloyd Hundling who also died in the accident.

SELECTED RECORDS

'Charlie Barnet and his Orchestra'	DJM Records	DJML 061
'Charlie Barnet 1939—41' Vol. 1	Black and White RCA	PM 42041

Frank Evans

COURTESY BLUE BAG RECORDS

FRANK EVANS

Born—Bristol, England

1st October 1936

Frank Evans

Frank Evans began playing the guitar at the age of 11. His early jazz influences were Charlie Christian and Django Reinhardt, although over the years he has studied a much broader spectrum of music including Classical and Eastern styles.

His early years as a professional guitarist were spent working in restaurants and clubs playing mainly standards. He did spend many years on the road in Britain and Europe with several jazz groups, including one led by saxophonist Tubby Hayes, but decided to settle permanently in his home town of Bristol since 1965—6.

Today Frank Evans is very involved in the Bristol music scene, writing and arranging for television and other commercial work, but also devoting much of his time to playing jazz in local clubs. He runs his own recording studio and has made several records which have proved very popular and there is no doubt these have made many British guitarists more aware of the great and legendary jazz guitarists of past and present.

SELECTED RECORDS

'Jazz Tete a Tete' (with Tubby Hayes)	77 Records	77LEU
'Mark Twain Suite'	77 Records	77SEU
'In an English Manner'	Saydisc	SDL 233
'Stretching Forth'	Saydisc	SDL 217
'Noctuary'	Blue Bag	101
Soiree'	Blue Bag	102

COURTESY CONCORD RECORDS/PHOTO PHIL LINDSAY

Tal Farlow

TAL FARLOW

Born—TALMADGE HOLT FARLOW
Greensboro, North Carolina, U.S.A.

7th June 1921

Talmadge Holt Farlow set out to be a commercial painter and artist and did not start playing professionally until he was 22. But from the age of eight Tal had played the guitar as a hobby. His father played guitar, banjo, ukulele and violin and Tal taught himself on one of his father's instruments. It was in the 1940's that Tal first heard Charlie Christian on some Benny Goodman records and immediately started playing as like Christian as he could, listening to the records over and over again until he could play Christian's guitar solos note for note. Until 1943 music was still to be a hobby for Tal and sign painting was his profession, but with the establishment of a large Army Air Force training base at Greensboro there was a sudden demand for musicians to play at the U.S.O. dances. One of the many musicians that Tal played with at these was Jimmy Lyons the jazz pianist. After the war Farlow joined a group led by the well-known female pianist Dardanelle, playing at the 'Copacabana' nightspot in New York for six months. During this period Tal was exposed to the sounds of Charlie Parker, Dizzy Gillespie and other leaders of the modern jazz/bop movement. His first real break came when Red Norvo was looking for a replacement for Mundell Lowe in his trio, Mundell recommended Tal for the job and so the new Red Norvo trio consisted of Red on vibraphone, Tal on guitar, and Red Kelly on double bass. It was this period with the Norvo trio that Tal attributed to the achievement of the extraordinary fast technique that he now has.

Red Norvo's trio became established as one of the most popular sounds in jazz of the fifties, with their recordings constantly amongst the best selling records. Tal appeared with this trio on the first ever colour television programme and it was then that he was fully recognized not only for unbelievably fast technique but for the brilliance of his improvisations and musical concept. Playing an instrument of his own design with a finger board over an inch shorter than the standard pattern Tal achieved a most individual sound, recognized by its softness of tone in comparison to his contemporaries. Whilst with the Norvo trio he developed various original rhythm techniques often confusing listeners into thinking that a drummer had been added to the line-up. He was able to play chords whilst tapping out rhythm on the guitar body and strings with his finger tips.

In 1954 Farlow won the 'Downbeat' New Star Award and in 1956 the 'Downbeat' critics' poll. By this time Tal was now recognized world-wide as one of America's leading jazz artists and he recorded several LP's under his own name with such stars as Ray Brown, Chico Hamilton, Eddie Costa, Vinnie Burke and Stan Levey.

In 1958 Tal married and that year also marked what was to be his last important public appearance for several years. It was held at the 'Composer' club in Manhattan. He moved to a new home in Sea Bright, New Jersey, on the Atlantic coast and entered virtual semi-retirement spending much of his time at his old love sign painting. Nevertheless he did not neglect his playing entirely and from time to time many of the world's top guitarists took time off to visit him, play and talk guitar. In 1968 Tal made a brief comeback appearing to packed houses for seven weeks, with his trio, at the 'Frammis' club on Manhattan's East Side.

After this brief reappearance in 1968 Tal Farlow returned again to semi-retirement as a professional musician at his home in Sea Bright. Pressure from jazz lovers plus his own desire to play has fortunately encouraged Tal since 1975 to play again regularly. He is now once more recording, giving concerts and sessions in local jazz clubs, and also working on a guitar method for 'Guitar Player Productions'.

SELECTED RECORDS
'Red Norvo Trio' (2 lp's)   Savoy
'Tal Farlow Quartet'   Blue Note

'Harold Arlen' by Tal Farlow	Verve	CLP 1439
'Tal Farlow Album'	Norgran	1047
'Interpretations of Tal Farlow'	Norgran	1027
'Recital by Tal Farlow'	Norgran	1030
'Guitar Artistry of Tal Farlow'	Verve	6143
'Swing Guitars'	Norgran	1033
'Tal'	Verve	8021
'Swinging Guitar of Tal Farlow'	Columbia	CLP 10132
'This is Tal Farlow'	Verve	MGV 8289
'Autumn in New York'	Norgran	1097
'Tal Farlow—Fuerst Set'	Xanadu	109
'Tal Farlow—Second Set'	Xanadu	119
'Return of Tal Farlow'	Prestige	7732
'Sign of the Time'	Concord	CJ 26
'Mostly Flute' with Sam Most	Xanadu	133
'Tal Farlow Trio—Trinity'	CBS Sony	25AP 597

SELECTED READING

'Whatever happened to Tal Farlow'	Ira Gitler, 'Downbeat', 5th December 1963
'The Octopus Returns—Tal Farlow'	Mort Fega, 'Downbeat', 27th June 1968
'Tal Farlow, a Jazz Legend'	Robert Yelin, 'Guitar Player', June 1975

Tal Farlow

COURTESY XANADU RECORDS/PHOTO DON SCHLITTEN

AL GAFA

Born— ALEXANDER GAFA
Brooklyn, New York, U.S.A.

9th April 1941

Al Gafa

Al Gafa is a self taught player who began his first professional experience working as a rock musician in the studios in New York City from 1964—9. He played with a wide variety of musicians and singers such as Sammy Davis Jnr. and from 1970—1 he was musical director for Carmen McRae. In 1971 he joined the Dizzy Gillespie sextet and it was then that he gained his first prominence as a jazz soloist and composer. He currently still works most of his time around New York City in the studios and jazz clubs and in 1976 made his first record as leader. This has been released on the Pablo label.

SELECTED RECORDS

'Bahiana'—Dizzy Gillespie Quintet	Pablo	2625—708
'Leblon Beach' Al Gafa Quintets	Pablo	2310—782

SELECTED READING

'Pro's Reply'	Al Gafa—'Guitar Player', May, September 1976

Al Gafa with the Dizzy Gillespie Quintet.

SLIM GAILLARD

Born— **BULEE GAILLARD** Detroit, Michigan, U.S.A.

4th January 1916

Slim Gaillard and his Trio.

A multi-instrumentalist, Slim Gaillard gained prominence on the jazz scene in the late thirties as a vocalist/guitarist in a duo with bassist Slam Stewart. Slim and Slam achieved great popularity and Gaillard's bop-influenced guitar playing, though of limited ability gained him recording dates with jazzmen of the calibre of Charlie Parker and Dizzy Gillespie. He was also featured in several films on guitar.

Slim's father was a merchant sailor and during the school holidays Slim was sometimes taken along on his boat trips. By the time he was in his early twenties Gaillard was working solo as a tap dancer and guitarist in variety. In 1937 he moved to New York and after appearing in a radio talent show he joined up with Slam Stewart. Their composition 'Flat Foot Floogie' became a best seller and assured the duo success until Slim joined the Army in 1943. He was released from the Army in 1944 and he worked and lived in the Los Angeles area, leading his own groups in various clubs. The next twenty years were to find Slim working outside of jazz as vocalist/comedian and even for a time in 1962 as a motel manager.

In recent years Gaillard has continued working as a cabaret artist, sometimes with his own band, but more often as a solo pianist. He had had a brief reunion with Slam Stewart at the Monterey Jazz Festival in 1970.

SELECTED RECORDS

'Slim and Slam' Vol. 1	Caete	LP—3
'Slim and Slam' Vol. 2	Caete	LP—4
'Slim and Slam'	Tax	M—8028
'Slim Gaillard and Friends'	Storyville	SLP 809
'Son of McVouty'	Hep	11
'Slims Jam 1945—6'	Alamac	QSR 2441
'Slim Gaillard Rides Again'	Paramount	CO64—924 87

SELECTED READING

'Found—Slim Gaillard'	Bob Horne, 'Downbeat', 27th June 1968

BARRY GALBRAITH

Born— JOSEPH BARRY GALBRAITH
Pittsburgh, Pennsylvania, U.S.A.

18th December 1919

Barry Galbraith

COURTESY GUITAR PLAYER

Barry Galbraith originally started as a banjoist, but hearing the guitar artistry of Eddie Lang, backing vocalist Bing Crosby in the early nineteen thirties, he changed over to the six stringed instrument.

Self taught, Galbraith gained his first professional experience playing in clubs around Pittsburgh. He played with many top jazz stars such as Red Norvo and Teddy Powell but his first major professional success was in New York as guitarist with the Claude Thornhill Band from 1941—2 and then again in 1946—7 after he had served in the Army.

From 1947—70 Barry spent most of his time as one of the most highly respected staff musicians working for the NBC and CBS networks. He developed a high reputation and as such was involved as a sideman on literally hundreds of recordings. The artists he has played with could read like 'Who's Who of Jazz' and popular music, Stan Kenton, Peggy Lee, Ella Fitzgerald, Tony Bennet, Benny Goodman, are only a few of the names with which Barry Galbraith has been featured.

In recent times this fine guitarist has unfortunately suffered from a severe back complaint and has involved himself mainly in private teaching in New York and also as a faculty member at New York City College.

SELECTED RECORDS

'East Coast Jazz No. 8 with Hal McCusick'	Bethlehem	39
'Tal Farlow Album'	Norgran	1047
'Guitar and the Wind'	Decca	9200

SELECTED READING

'Barry Galbraith—A Life in Jazz'	Arnie Berle, 'Guitar Player', July 1976

DICK GARCIA

Born— **RICHARD JOSEPH GARCIA**
New York City, U.S.A.

11th May 1931

Dick Garcia

Dick Garcia started playing the guitar at the age of nine. His father and grandfather were guitarists, and his great-grandfather reputedly once played the guitar in a command performance for the King of Spain.

Virtually self taught Garcia's first professional break came when vibist Terry Gibbs heard him in a jam session in Greenwich Village. Gibbs recommended him to clarinettist Tony Scott with whom Garcia was to play throughout 1950. He then played with various groups including almost a year with the George Shearing Quintet in 1952. From 1955–6 Garcia once more played with Tony Scott and then again with Shearing in 1959. Although a very able soloist, Garcia has now dropped out of the limelight and is occupied mainly in freelance work in and around New York.

SELECTED RECORDS

'The Hi-fi land of Jazz'	Seeco	CELP 428
'Message from Garcia'	Dawn	1106
'Fourmost Guitars'	ABC	109

Dick Garcia with the George Shearing Quintet.

HANK GARLAND

Born—Orangeburg, South Carolina, U.S.A.

11th November 1930

Hank Garland

COURTESY C. E. H. SMITH

Originally a banjo player, Hank Garland changed to the guitar and was soon a featured soloist in several country and western bands in the Nashville area. Hank became the lead guitarist with the popular Paul Howard band in the late nineteen forties. For many years he was regarded only as a country style guitar picker, his jazz playing was reserved for small clubs in Nashville.

In 1960 he made what was to be his only real jazz record with vibist Gary Burton, bassist Joe Benjamin, and drummer Joe Morello. This record proved that Garland was destined to be a top line jazz soloist. Unfortunately shortly after this recording session Garland was involved in a serious car crash that has left him disabled, and so unable to continue his career as a guitarist.

SELECTED RECORDS
'Jazz Winds from a New Direction'	Philips	SBBL 622
'Nashville All Stars'	RCA	2302

ARV GARRISON

Born— ARVIN CHARLES GARRISON Toledo, Ohio, U.S.A.
17th August 1922

Died—Toledo, Ohio, U.S.A. 30th July 1960

Arv Garrison (left), other guitarists are Barney Kessel, Tony Rizzi, Irving Ashby and Gene Sargent.

COURTESY CHARLES E. H. SMITH

Arv Garrison started on the ukulele at the age of nine but changed to the guitar at 12. His first playing experience was with high school bands in which he played until he was 18 years old.

In 1941 he was fronting his own group in Albany, New York. From late 1941 after playing with Don Seat in Pittsburgh, through to 1948 Garrison played on both the West and East coasts with his own trio developing a high reputation as a jazz guitarist amongst his fellow musicians. In 1946 he married bassist Vivien Garry. In the nineteen fifties Garrison returned to his home town of Toledo where he continued his guitar playing, but out of the public limelight, until his death in 1960.

SELECTED RECORDS		
'Giants of Modern Jazz'	Explosive	528–013
'Howard McGee Sextet'	Spotlite	SPJ–131
'Charlie Parker on Dial'	Spotlite	101

JIMMY GOURLEY

Born—JAMES PASCO GOURLEY JNR.
St. Louis, Missouri, U.S.A.

9th June 1926

Jimmy Gourley with Kenny Clarke and Lou Bennet.

Jimmy Gourley started playing the guitar at the age of 10. His father had founded the Conservatory of Music in Hammond, Indiana.

One of Jimmy's first jazz sessions at school was with saxophonist Lee Konitz in 1941. He gained valuable experience with the Navy Band from 1944–6. From 1946–8 he replaced Jimmy Raney in the Chicago band led by Jay Burkhart and stayed with this outfit for two years. Gourley's style of playing in fact has always reflected a strong Raney influence.

After leaving Burkhart Gourley freelanced with various jazz artists including Sonny Stitt, Gene Ammons and Anita O'Day. In 1951 he decided to move to Europe and he joined forces with Henri Renaud with whom he played until 1954. Whilst in Europe he recorded with many visiting U.S. musicians including Zoot Sims, Lee Konitz, Bob

Brookmeyer and Clifford Brown.

In 1956 the guitarist returned to U.S.A. and played for a short while with bassist Chubby Jackson in Chicago. In December 1957 he decided to take up residence once more in Paris, where he has since spent most of his time.

Jimmy Gourley was featured as a regular artist at the top Parisian jazz club 'The Blue Note' from 1959–65, usually with drummer Kenny Clarke. He led his own quartet on tour throughout Switzerland and Italy and also at the Parisian club 'Chat Qui Peche'. From 1970–2 he jointly ran a jazz club 'The Half Note' in the Canary Islands but this closed as a jazz club in April 1972 and Gourley returned once more to Paris to play at the 'Club St. Germain'. He continues playing and recording in and around Paris although he did appear in 1975 at 'Sweet Basil's club in New York.

SELECTED RECORDS

'Stephane Grapelli' (2 lp's)	Festival	FLD 596
'Lou Bennet Quartet'	RCA Camden	900–078
'Americans in Europe Vol. 1'	Impulse	AS 36
'Graffiti'	Promophone	14

COURTESY MELODY MAKER/PHOTO HERVE DERRIEN

A galaxy of French Guitarists. Left to Right: Sacha Distel, Jean Pierre Sassoon, Jimmy Gourley, Henri Krola, Jean Bonnal.

FREDDIE GREEN

Born—FREDERICK WILLIAM GREEN
Charleston, South Carolina, U.S.A.

31st March 1911

Freddie Green

Freddie Green has proved to be one of the most unique guitarists in jazz history. He is the undisputed king of the rhythm guitar as opposed to the solo guitar. His fantastic rhythm guitar playing has been the backbone of the legendary Count Basie band since 1937, and in fact, in many jazz lovers' opinions the sound of his guitar is as much the Count Basie sound as the Count's unique piano style.

At the age of 12 Freddie Green moved from Carolina to New York City where he began to teach himself music and the guitar. John Hammond had heard him play in a Greenwich Village club and recommended him to Count Basie. Since then Freddie has played continually with the Basie band, setting unsurpassed standards in the art of rhythm guitar. Except for one or two bars of obligato chords, he has never taken a solo with the Basie band, and he has never played the electric guitar. Yet his unique ability is a legend in jazz, and has left its mark on virtually every Count Basie recording, as well as being much in demand for recordings by many other top jazzmen including Lester Young, Lionel Hampton, Benny Carter and Benny Goodman.

SELECTED RECORDS
*'Pee Wee Russell's Rhythm Makers 1938'	BYG	529—066
'Chairman of the Board' (Basie Band)	Roulette	52032
'Rhythm Willie' (with Herb Ellis)	Concord	CJ 10
'Mr. Rhythm'	French RCA	PM 42114

*Freddie Green plays a sixteen bar rhythmic chord solo on the track 'Dinah' on this record.

SUGGESTED READING
'The Tough Straight Art—Rhythm Guitar'	Tom Scanlan—'Downbeat', 1st July 1965

GRANT GREEN

Born—St. Louis, Missouri, U.S.A.

6th June 1931

Grant Green

Grant Green first learnt the guitar whilst at school, and at the age of 13 was already a professional musician. He devoted his energies initially to Boogie Woogie and then Rock and Roll but he soon fell under the influence of jazz saxophonists Lester Young and Charlie Parker.

In the early 1960's tenor saxophonist Lou Donaldson heard Green playing in a St. Louis club and encouraged him to come to New York to play. Donaldson persuaded the Blue Note Record Company to record the young guitarist, and as a result Grant received many rave reviews for his playing from jazz critics. He was hailed as the new

heir to Charlie Christian's throne. Grant became the staff guitarist for Blue Note and he soon broadened his musical experience by recording regularly with a wide variety of top jazz artists including Jimmy Smith, Stanley Turrentine, and Herbie Hancock.

He also recorded many fine albums under his own name for Blue Note, and these particularly emphasise his swinging, single note guitar style. Green continued to play in clubs in and around New York but dropped out of the scene from 1967—9 due to personal problems. In 1970 he moved to Detroit where he is now based.

SELECTED RECORDS

'Grant's first Stand'	Blue Note	4064
'Green Street'	Blue Note	4071
'Grantstand'	Blue Note	4086
'Sunday Mornin''	Blue Note	4099
'Talking About'	Blue Note	4183
'Visions'	Blue Note	4373
'Iron City'	Cobblestone	9002

SELECTED READING

'Grant Green—New Guitar in Town'	Dan Morganstern—'Downbeat', 19th July 1952
'Grant Green'	Gary N. Bourland—'Guitar Player', January 1975

TINY GRIMES

Born— LLOYD GRIMES
Newport News, Virginia, U.S.A.

7th July 1917

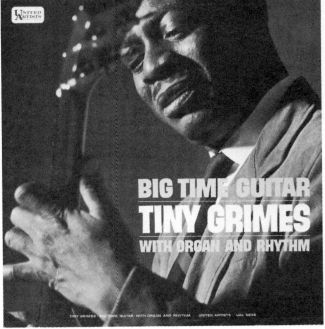

Tiny Grimes

Originally a drummer, having played in the high school band, Tiny Grimes started his musical career on the piano in Washington D.C. in 1935. In 1938 he moved to New York City where he played at the 'Rhythm Club'. He taught himself to play the electric four string guitar, an instrument originally devised to ease the transition of banjo players to the guitar, and in 1940 he was featured with a group called the 'Cats and a Fiddle'.

In 1941 he moved to California where during a jam session he met Art Tatum. The pianist was so impressed with Grimes' playing that he invited him to complete his trio with bassist Slam Stewart. After three historical years with Tatum, the guitarist formed his own group in New York City called the 'Rocking Highlanders'. This proved quite popular but in 1947 he moved to Cleveland, and later in the fifties settled in Philadelphia. He returned in the sixties to New York City where he played regularly in Harlem and Greenwich Village. His swinging, bluesy playing became much appreciated in Europe, in particular in France, after his tours in 1968 with organist Milt Buckner and later in 1970 with Jay McShann. In the last few years his individual guitar sound has been in constant demand on the East Coast of the U.S.A., both in jazz clubs and at festivals. He has recently recorded with trumpeter Roy Eldridge in New York.

SELECTED RECORDS

'Tiny in Swingville'	Prestige	2002
'Big Time Guitar'	United Artists	VAL 3232
'Tiny Grimes and his Rocking Highlanders'	Riverboat	900—2101
'Tiny Grimes—Some Groovy Fours'	Black and Blue	33—067
'Tiny Grimes and Roy Eldridge'	Sonet	SNTF 736

SELECTED READING

'A Tribute to Tiny Grimes'	Hugh Panassie—'Downbeat', 26th July 1969

MARTY GROSZ

Born—Berlin, Germany

28th February 1930

Marty Grosz

Marty Grosz has come to the fore in recent years as a fine acoustic guitar player. He is not only a rhythm player but also a soloist carrying on the tradition and styles of Dick McDonough, Carl Kress, George Van Eps and other top acoustic players of the nineteen thirties.

Grosz's father was a famous satirical artist in Germany before World War II. With the rise of the Nazi party he left Germany in 1933 to settle in the U.S.A., making his home in New York. Marty started to play the ukulele at the age of eight but did not take up the guitar until he was 12. He became interested in jazz, in particular Chicago style, and he played later with various groups around New York.

In 1954, on leaving the Army, Marty settled in Chicago where he took up the banjo. Over the next few years he played in a wide variety of jobs, usually on the banjo. Always fascinated by the guitar, he experimented with many tunings in his spare time. He ended up with one, based on a banjo tuning, not unlike the one used by Carl Kress.

He first came to national prominence in 1974 when saxophonist Bob Wilber asked him to join the 'Soprano Summit'. The relatively enormous success of this group, both in concert and on record, has brought to the attention of the world's jazz listeners the talents of Marty Grosz.

Marty now lives in New York. He plays a good portion of the year with the 'Soprano Summit' in the U.S.A. and in other countries of the world. Of recent he has been featured in a new guitar duo with Wayne Wright. The bulk of their repertoire is based on popular acoustic guitar solos and duets from the nineteen thirties.

There is no doubt that Grosz has made an important contribution to the jazz guitar. He has brought to the attention of thousands of guitarists the jazz artistry of the early acoustic guitar players. The result has been a new interest in a field of the jazz guitar which to a large extent had been forgotten.

SELECTED RECORDS

'Soprano Summit'	Concord	CJ 29
'Chalumeau Blue'	Chiaroscuru	CR 148
'Let Your Fingers do the Walking'	Aviva	6000
'Take me to the Land of Jazz'	Aviva	6001

SELECTED READING

'Marty Grosz'	'Coda' Magazine, February 1977
'Marty Grosz'	Dan Forte, 'Guitar Player', March 1978

FRED GUY

Born—FREDERICK GUY Burkeville, Galveston, U.S.A.
23rd May 1899

Died—Chicago, U.S.A. 22 November 1971

Fred Guy with the Duke Ellington Orchestra 1935.

Originally starting his career as a banjoist, Fred Guy changed to the guitar in 1933. The main reason for his inclusion in this book is that he was with the Duke Ellington orchestra with hardly a break from its conception in the twenties until 1947. Like Freddie Green, he was a rhythm player and an integral part of the Duke's original rhythm section. When he left the orchestra in 1947 he was never replaced by Ellington.

After he quit playing with the Duke, Guy gave up music and became a ballroom manager in Chicago where at the age of 72 he committed suicide.

SELECTED RECORDS

'Duke Ellington on V. Discs'	Jazz Live	BLJ 8018
'Duke Ellington Cotton Club 1938'	Jazz Anthology	30JA 5169
'Duke Ellington Original Session 1943—5'	Jazz Anthology	30JA 5103
'Duke Ellington Live Session 1943—5'	Jazz Anthology	30JA 5124

JERRY HAHN

Born– JERRY DONALD HAHN
Alma, Nebraska, U.S.A.

21st September 1940

Jerry Hahn

COURTESY GUITAR PLAYER

When Jerry reached the age of seven, the Hahn family moved to Wichita, Kansas. Influenced by his father and uncle, both steel guitar players, Jerry started playing originally on the steel guitar. By the time he was in his late teens Jerry was already playing with various local bands and had made the change to a regular six string guitar. Influenced at that time by West coast jazz guitarists, in particular Barney Kessel, Jerry turned his attention to jazz rather than country music. In 1962 he moved to San Francisco where he initially played in bars and hotels.

Jerry's first important jazz date was when he joined alto-saxophonist John Handy in 1964. Appearing with Handy at the Monterey Jazz Festival in 1965, Jerry drew much admiration from jazz lovers for his part in that group. In 1968 he joined the brilliant young vibist, Gary Burton, with whom he toured the world for the good part of a year. He then formed his own group in 1970 called the 'Jerry Hahn Brotherhood'. But in 1971 personal problems, due to his divorce, caused him to alter his style of life.

Since 1972 he has held the position of Professor in music at Wichita State University, and he also cooperates on various projects for the Conn Musical Instruments Co. for whom he sometimes demonstrates. Jerry is also a regular contributor in the magazine 'Guitar Player', and his columns are recommended reading for any guitarist interested in jazz.

SELECTED RECORDS

'John Handy Album–2'	CBS	BPG 62881
'Jerry Hahn Quintet'	Arhoolie	8006
'Are-Be-In'	Changes	LP 7001
'Brotherland'	Columbia	CS 1044
'Moses'	Fantasy	9426

SELECTED READING

'Brotherhood to Moses'	Ron Crotty–'Downbeat', 7th June 1973
'Jerry Hahn'	Jim Crockett–'Guitar Player', March 1971

JIM HALL

Born – JAMES STANLEY HALL
Buffalo, New York State, U.S.A.

4th December 1930

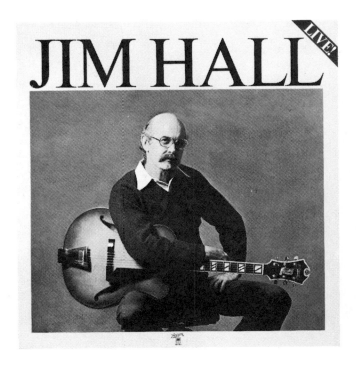

Jim Hall as a child was surrounded by music, as his grandfather played the violin, his mother the piano, and his uncle the guitar. It was the uncle who influenced Jim to take up the guitar at the age of 10 Jim began taking lessons. His talent was soon evident and although it was against union rules, he was playing in dance bands professionally at the age of 13. Like many of today's other jazz guitar greats, it was the sounds of Charlie Christian that first turned Jim Hall's attention to jazz.

When he was 16, Hall's family moved to Cleveland where he later obtained a degree from the Cleveland Institute of Music. It was during this period that Jim became conscious of the gypsy guitar genius, Django Reinhardt, and this obviously affected the further development of his guitar style. Not happy with economic prospects as a guitarist in Cleveland, he decided to move to Los Angeles where he felt he could both earn a living and still continue his musical studies at the U.C.L.A.

In 1958, famed jazz drummer, Chico Hamilton was forming what was to be his first outstanding Quintet. John Grass, the late french horn player, recommended Hall. Jim subsequently got the job with this highly successful group, staying with it for one-and-a-half years. This was to be his first step up the ladder to the top of the jazz guitar tree. At the end of 1959, he joined another highly successful small group, the Jimmy Giuffre trio which was as equally innovative as the Hamilton group and Jim received well deserved praise for his part in it from jazz lovers and critics from all over the world.

Now established world-wide as a jazz musician of the highest calibre Jim was selected to play with singers such as Ella Fitzgerald and Yves Montand. As well as jazz artists such as Lee Konitz, Red Mitchell, Art Farmer, Bill Evans and Sonny Rollins. In many cases he produced some fine and historic recordings with these players.

During the middle sixties Hall hit hard times as jazz suffered a general loss in popularity. But since the beginning of the seventies, he has made a wonderful recovery back to the top. Over the past few years, he has made some really outstanding recordings with bassist Ron Carter, and various other artists. These rank amongst some of the best guitar music available on record and certainly confirm the title often bestowed upon him 'The Poet of Jazz'. Those who have heard him play recently rate him as one of today's most inventive and lyrical jazz musicians.

At the present time Jim Hall is based in New York, playing regularly at jazz festivals and various well-known jazz clubs. He has recorded for the Milestone label, the MPS label in Germany, and recently the Horizon and Choice record companies in the U.S.A.

SELECTED RECORDS

'Chico Hamilton Quintet'	Vogue	LAG 12045
'Jimmy Guiffre Three'	London	LTL–K 15130
'Jim Hall "Trio"'	Vogue	LAE 12072
'Undercurrent' (Duo with Bill Evans)	United Artists	VAJ 14003
'Intermodulation' (Duo with Bill Evans)	Verve	VLP 9145

'Street Swingers'	Vogue	LAC 12147
'Otra Vez'	Mainstream	MRL 358
'It's Nice to be with You'	MPS	20708
'Where would I Be'	Milestone	MSP 9037
'Alone Together' (Guitar/Bass Duets)	Milestone	MSP 9045
'Jim Hall Live'	Horizon A & M	SP—705
'Jim Hall Concierto'	CTI Records	CTI 606051
'Jim Hall Commitment'	Horizon A & M	SP—715

SELECTED READING

'The Musical Philosophy of Jim Hall'	Bill Coss—'Downbeat', 19th July 1962
'Unassuming Jim Hall'	Don Nelsen—'Downbeat', 1st July 1965
'Jim Hall—Quiet Strength'	Jane Welch—'Downbeat', 10th June 1971
'Jim Hall'	An Interview—'Guitar Player', March 1970
'Jim Hall—Ever Changing'	Leonard Ferris—'Guitar Player', April 1974

Jim Hall

COURTESY CRESCENDO/PHOTO DENNIS MATHEWS

BILL HARRIS

Born—WILLIE HARRIS
Nashville, North Carolina, U.S.A.

14th April 1925

Bill Harris

COURTESY GUITAR PLAYER

As a child Bill Harris was taught the piano by his mother and he was later to play the organ in his father's church. He was given a guitar by his uncle on his twelfth birthday but soon gave it up as he did not make much progress. It was eight years later, on his discharge from the army, that Bill decided to take up the guitar seriously.

Initially Bill played the plectrum guitar and played classical pieces for his own enjoyment with a pick, but whilst studying at the Columbia School of Music in Washington, Sophocles Papas encouraged him to try the classical guitar.

Bill made his living gigging in and around Washington with various groups, and whilst playing with a rhythm and blues vocal group, he was heard by Mickey Baker who encouraged him to make his first solo record in 1958 on the nylon string guitar. This proved quite successful, being probably the first solo jazz guitar record played on the classical guitar. It was obviously an early influence on Charlie Byrd, whose world-wide success followed very shortly after this record's release.

Bill Harris has never made the big time in jazz, but contents himself today with teaching in his own school in Washington D.C. occasionally recording and doing session work on the East Coast.

SELECTED RECORDS

'The Harris Touch'	Emarcy	MG 36113
'Great Guitar Sounds'	Mercury	MGW 16220
'Down in the Alley'	Black and Blue	33—042
'Rhythm'	Black and Blue	33—062

SELECTED MUSIC

'Classic Jazz'	Bill Harris Publications
'Instant Guitar'	Bill Harris Publications
'Harris Touch'	Bill Harris Publications

SELECTED READING

'Introducing Bill Harris'	Pete Welding—'Jazz Journal' NOvember 1960
'Bill Harris'	Pete Welding—'Downbeat', 20th July 1961
'Acoustic Maverick'	Bill McLarney—'Downbeat', 27th June 1968
'Bill Harris'	Jerry Dullman—'Guitar Player' May 1975

AL HENDRICKSON

Born – ALTON REYNOLDS HENDRICKSON
Eastland, Texas, U.S.A.

10th May 1920

Although not widely known today to the general jazz listener, Al Hendrickson is highly respected by fellow jazz guitarists in the U.S.A. Today he is regarded as one of the top studio guitarists in the Hollywood studios.

Al first came to prominence in the Artie Shaw band and 'Gramercy Five' from 1942–5. Later he was singer/guitarist with the Benny Goodman band and sextet. Over a period of many years he was the first choice as guitarist for bands such as Ray Noble, Woody Herman, Johnny Mandel and Neal Hefti. He was also featured in the 1962 Monterey

Jazz Festival with top jazzmen Dizzy Gillespie and Louis Bellson, Al Hendrickson's guitar playing can be heard in a multitude of recordings with these and other artists, including the guitar groups 'Guitars Inc' and 'Guitars Unlimited'.

Other artists with whom Al has been associated include Nat Cole, Peggy Lee, Gordon Jenkins, Frank Sinatra, Benny Carter, Lalo Schifrin, Nelson Riddle, Phil Moore, Lena Horne, and Quincy Jones.

He is currently recording for films and television, as well as writing guitar music and methods for the Mel Bay Publishing Company.

SELECTED RECORDS

Barney Kessel 'To Swing or not to Swing'	Contemporary	3513
Guitars Inc—"Invitation'	Warner Bros.	1206
Guitars Inc—'Soft and Subtle'	Warner Bros.	1246
Guitars Unlimited 'Tender is the Night'	Capitol	ST 173
Dizzy Gillespie—'Big Band 1965'	Trip Jazz	TRLP 5584
'Juggernaut'	Concord	CJ 40

SELECTED MUSIC

'Jazz Guitar Duets'	Mel Bay Publications

MICHAEL HOWELL

Born—Kansas City, Missouri, U.S.A.

8th October 1943

Michael Howell

Michael Howell was first taught the guitar by his father at the age of seven and he continued his studies with a local musician, Herley Dennis. Michael received his degree in musical education from Lamar Jnr. College in Colorado when he was 18.

Following this Michael decided to move to San Francisco where he studied at the local Music and Arts Institute. There he received his first jazz break with vibist Bobby Hutchinson and saxophonist Harold Land in 1971. Since that time he has played with many top line jazz players, including Sonny Rollins, Dizzy Gillespie and John Handy, gathering a fine reputation for his guitar work on his way.

He regards Wes Montgomery and Charlie Parker as his most important influences and many jazz critics regard him as one of the most promising of the young guitarists on the scene today. He has recently recorded with his own groups on the Milestone label.

SELECTED RECORDS
'In the Looking Glass'	Milestone	M9048
'In the Silence'	Milestone	M9054
'Alone'	Catalyst	CAT 7615

SELECTED READING
'Michael Howell—Finger Style Jazz' Len Lyons—'Guitar Player', April 1975
'Michael Howell—A Profile' Len Lyons—'Downbeat' 13th March 1975

COURTESY CSL

Ike Isaacs

IKE ISAACS

Born—ISAAC ISAACS
Rangoon, Burma

1st December 1919

Ike Isaacs is recognized as one of the foremost plectrum guitarists in the world today, one of the few living outside of America. Although much of his time is spent in the television and recording studios Ike still plays jazz weekly in various groups in the London area. He also devotes a considerable amount of time to writing and arranging for the guitar.

Ike began playing the guitar at the age of 14. Although Ike comes from a very musical family, he originally played only as a hobby for he was pursuing a degree in chemistry at Rangoon University. In 1942 he graduated with a B.Sc., but due to the war was forced to move to India. There he was assigned to a government factory as a storekeeper. In order to prop up his low wages Ike worked as a musician whenever possible in local hotels.

After the war, in 1946, Ike moved to London as he had now decided to make music and the guitar his career. He soon got his first job with the ex-Bomber Command band led by Leslie Douglas. Ike left Douglas in 1947 and joined the group playing at Hatchetts Restaurant in Piccadilly. He was also the featured guitarist with the BBC radio showband for some time.

His first real prominence to jazz guitarists in Britain came when he was featured on the highly successful BBC radio programme 'Guitar Club'. This programme was broadcast every Saturday evening and Ike led the resident guitar group.

For many years Ike spent much of his time away from the jazz scene, although he did record with groups like the Ted Heath Band. He was sought after by the television, film and radio studios alike and so he had little time for playing jazz. In 1975 Ike was offered a position with the Stephane Grapelli quartet, an offer Ike decided to take and for two years he toured the world with the famous violinist for an extended break from the grind of studio work.

Since early 1977 Ike has settled once more at his home in London and now shares his time between the studios, various jazz gigs, and writing new works for the guitar. He regularly contributes an excellent jazz guitar column in the British magazine 'Crescendo'. Ike's musicianship is renowned throughout the guitar world and as a result he is usually the first call for top line guitarists when they visit London.

SELECTED RECORDS

'Guitar Club'	Saga (3EPS)	ESAG 7001/2/3
'I Like Ike'	Morgan	MR 116P
'Fourteen TV Themes'	Decca/Eclipse	ECS 2163
'I Love Paris'	Chapter One	LRP 5009
'Violinspiration' with Grapelli quartet	MPS/BASF	MPS 20 22545—3

SELECTED MUSIC

'Guitar Moods'	Kadence Music Co.
'Ibanez Guitar Album'	Kadence Music Co.
'Glen Miller for Guitar'	EMI Music Publishing Co.

SELECTED READING

'Ike Isaacs'	John Dalton—'Guitar', December 1977
'Guitar Column'	Ike Isaacs—'Crescendo' magazine (monthly)
'Ike Isaacs'	Joe Bivona—'Guitar Player', November 1976

Lonnie Johnson

COURTESY GUITAR MAGAZINE

LONNIE JOHNSON

Born—ALONZO JOHNSON New Orleans, U.S.A.
8th February 1889 (Not proven)

Died—Toronto, Canada, 16th June 1970

Lonnie Johnson

Lonnie Johnson was probably one of the greatest jazz guitarists the world has known. Fortunately due to the re-release on long playing records of many of his old recordings, particularly his duets with Eddie Lang, guitar and jazz lovers can today fully appreciate his genius. The influence on guitarists, right through to the present day of his bluesy and swinging guitar style is undisputed. He was also an authentic vocalist in the blues tradition and made many fine vocal recordings.

As a child Lonnie studied the violin, playing it in local theatres with his brother James, who was a pianist. He continued his professional career playing with riverboat bands and first came to nationwide prominence in 1925 when he won a blues contest in St. Louis, where he was living. Part of the contest prize was a contract for the 'Okeh' label and he made many records both in New York City and Chicago. His most outstanding tracks at that time were probably made with Eddie Lang but he was also featured with Duke Ellington and Louis Armstrong, amongst many others.

In 1932 through to 1937 he played with the Putney Dandridge orchestra in Cleveland and was featured occasionally on the radio. From 1937—40 Lonnie was continually working with artists such as Jimmy Noone and Johnny Dodds, but his brilliance was not fully exposed with these groups.

In 1940 he took up the electric guitar but his guitar style was not as convincing on the amplified instrument. Tragically his career musically declined from this point although he was playing regularly until 1952, At one time in 1958 he was forced to make his living as a chef in a Philadelphia hotel. Fortunately Lonnie was rediscovered by enthusiasts in the sixties, and he started recording and playing at jazz clubs once more. In early 1968 he appeared with the Duke Ellington Orchestra in New York, and in the autumn he toured Europe and Great Britain as part of a Blues package. Lonnie Johnson finally decided to settle in Toronto, where he was very popular with local blues fans. It was here that he died of a heart attack in 1970, the final result of a severe accident in 1969.

SELECTED RECORDS

'Blue Guitars' Vol. 1	Parlophone	PMC 7019
'Blue Guitars' Vol. 2	Parlophone	PMC 7106
'Stringing the Blues'	CBS	BPG 62143
'Pioneers of Jazz Guitar'	Yazoo	1057
'Eddie Lang—Jazz Guitar Virtuoso'	Yazoo	1059
'Lonnie Johnson—Live in Copenhagen'	Storyville	671—162
'Lonnie Johnson'	Xtra	1037

SELECTED READING

'The Devil's Music'	Giles Oakley p. 177—182, BBC Publications 1976
'Big Bill Blues'	Yannick Bruynoghe p. 92—94, Cassell 1955
'I Remember Lonnie'	Verum Clapp—'Jazz Journal', January 1972

COURTESY PHL ASSOCIATES

Barney Kessel

BARNEY KESSEL

Born—Muskogee, Oklahoma, U.S.A.

17th October 1923

Barney Kessel's parents were not keen on music, particularly as far as their son was concerned. But by the time he was 12, music and the guitar were the passion of Barney's life. Selling newspapers, he had soon saved enough to buy his first guitar. Although Barney received a few basic guitar lessons at school he was virtually self taught. At 14 he was the only white musician playing in an all-negro band in Muskogee.

In 1939 Barney's reputation was already so great that Charlie Christian came to hear Barney play when he was in Oklahoma City visiting his family. Meeting and playing with Charlie Christian strengthened Barney's determination to be a professional musician, and in 1942 he made his way to Hollywood.

Barney's Hollywood career began as a dishwasher, but his terrific talent on the guitar shone through, and he soon had the guitarist's chair in the Chico Marx orchestra, led at that time by drummer Ben Pollack. After a year of touring, Barney settled in Los Angeles, where he became the number-one guitarist on the radio networks. He appeared in the historic jazz film 'Jammin' the Blues' (1944)—the only white musician to have this honour. Over the next few years he played with many famous big bands, including those of Charlie Barnet, Artie Shaw, Benny Goodman, Hal McIntyre and Shorty Rogers. An opportunity came to join the Norman Granz 'Jazz at the Philharmonic' touring group in 1947. Longing to return to the jazz scene, Barney decided to take the opportunity. He toured and recorded with the Charlie Parker group, Sarah Vaughan and Lester Young.

In 1952 Barney joined the Oscar Peterson trio, which was to give him the world-wide recognition that repeatedly won him every leading jazz poll, including those of 'Downbeat', 'Metronome', 'Esquire', 'Melody Maker' and 'Playboy'.

Barney made a long-playing record under his own name in 1953 the first of nearly 40. Of all Barney's records which have been so influential to jazz guitarists, particularly outstanding are the original Poll Winner's albums with Shelley Manne on drums, and Ray Brown on bass. These records were historic in that they made the guitar, bass, and drums trio acceptable as a complete and individual sound, a great step forward in the evolution of the jazz guitar.

For many years Barney's talent was absorbed by the Hollywood studios. But in 1969 he gave up the very lucrative work in the film and television studios of Hollywood to dedicate himself to the music and the way of life he loves. He now spends much of his year touring the world jazz circuit, playing to capacity audiences wherever he goes. His guitar playing and musical genius have become a legend amongst guitarists and music lovers everywhere. The rest of his time he devotes to conducting his famous seminar, 'The Effective Guitarist' in many countries, making new records, and composing music. Barney also now writes a regular column in "Guitar Player' magazine and has also recently worked as an 'Ambassador of Jazz' for the U.S. State Department behind the Iron Curtain.

SELECTED RECORDS—For a fuller listing refer to 'A Living Legend' by M. J. Summerfield)

'Easy Like'	Contemporary	C3511
'Plays Standards'	Contemporary	C3512
'To Swing or not to Swing'	Contemporary	C3513
'The Poll Winners' No. 1	Contemporary	C3535
'Plays Carmen'	Contemporary	C3563
'Four'	Contemporary	C3026
'Music to Listen To'	Contemporary	C3521
'The Poll Winners Ride Again' No. 2	Contemporary	C3556
'Some Like it Hot'	Contemporary	C3565
'The Poll Winners Three' No. 3	Contemporary	C3576
'Workin' Out'	Contemporary	C3585
'Exploring the Scene' ('Poll Winners' No. 4)	Contemporary	C3581

'Let's Cook'	Contemporary	C3603
'Latin Rhythms'	Reprise	RP 6073
'Swinging Party'	Contemporary	C3613
'On Fire'	Emerald	2401
'Feeling Free'	Contemporary	C3618
'With Stephane Grapelli No. 1'	Polydor	2460 105
'With Stephane Grapelli No. 2'	Polydor	2460 173
'Swinging Easy'	Polydor	2460 130
'What's New'	Mercury	135 720
'Reflections of Rome'	RCA	34012
'Kessel's Kit'	RCA	SF 8098
'Jazz Portrait'	RCA	730710
'Summertime in Montreux'	Polydor	2460 210
'Two Way Conversation'	Sonet S LP	2550
'Just Friends'	Sonet SNTF	685
'Great Guitars' Vol. 1	Concord	4
'Barney Plays Kessel'	Concord	CJ−9
'Great Guitars' Vol. 2	Concord	CJ−23
'Poll Winners Straight Ahead'	Contemporary	S7635
'Soaring'	Concord	CJ−33
'Poor Butterfly' (duo with Herb Ellis)	Concord	CJ−34
'Kessel at Sometime—Japan'	Trio	PAP 9062

SELECTED MUSIC

'The Guitar'—A tutor	Barney Kessel, Windsor Music Co.
'Personal Manuscripts 1−6'	Barney Kessel, Windsor Music Co.
'West Coast Guitar'	Leeds Music Corp.

SELECTED READING

'A Living Legend'	Maurice J. Summerfield—'CSL Booklet' 1974
'Barney Kessel—The Versatile Guitarist'	John Tynan—'Downbeat', 24th July 1958
'Kessel Remembers Reinhardt'	John Tynan—'Downbeat', 25th June 1959
'Barney Kessel'	Discus, 'B.M.G.' August 1959
'Barney Kessel—Why he is back on the road'	Gene Lees—'Downbeat', 5th January 1961
'Barney Kessel 1966'	Harvey Siders—'Downbeat', 14th July 1966
'Kessel sur la Sellette'	'Jazz Magazine', April 1968
'Barney Kessel'	Bill Lee, 'Guitar Player', October 1970
'Kessel at Concord'	Bob Bangerter, 'Guitar Player', January/February 1973
'The Way Barney Kessel Sees It'	Les Tomkins, 'Crescendo', November 1972
'In Conversation' No. 1	Ike Isaacs, 'Guitar', December 1972
'In Conversation' No. 2	Ike Isaacs, 'Guitar', January 1973
'Barney Kessel'	George Clinton, 'Guitar', January 1977

Barney Kessel with Benny Carter and Ruby Braff.

COURTESY JAZZ JOURNAL/PHOTO MIKE DOYLE

EARL KLUGH

Born—Detroit, Michigan, U.S.A.

16th September 1953

Earl Klugh

Earl Klugh is a young guitarist recently introduced by poll winning guitarist/singer George Benson. He is now making records under his own name which are also having great commercial success.

Earl's first instrument was the piano but he started playing the guitar at 10. His first interest in the instrument was folk music and he followed the music of artists such as Peter, Paul and Mary. When he was 13 he heard some records by Chet Atkins and Klugh suddenly realized the full harmonic and melodic potential of the guitar. This discovery was emphasised when he heard the guitar artistry of George Van Eps.

Whilst teaching the guitar in a music store in Detroit he was heard by saxophonist Yusef Lateef. Lateef was so taken by the sixteen-year-old's jazz playing on the nylon string guitar that he gave him a spot on his album 'Suite 16' on the Atlantic label. The following year Klugh met George Benson in a Detroit night-club. Like Lateef, Benson was fascinated by the sound of Earl's classical guitar and together they worked out some duets. In 1973 Earl joined Benson's quartet and toured and recorded with him for a while.

Klugh was then approached by Chick Corea to join the popular 'Return to Forever' group on electric guitar. He did a national tour with this famous jazz/rock group which also featured Stanley Clarke and Lenny White. Following this tour the worked with singer Flora Purim and pianist George Shearing, which gave the young player a wide and varied exposure to top jazz music.

Today Earl is kept busy recording for Blue Note records which typify the young guitarist's individual approach to jazz and music as a whole. He has now made three albums, with varying groups under his own leadership. To date all have proved to be best sellers, which is quite an achievement for a twenty-four-year old.

SELECTED RECORDS

'White Rabbit' with George Benson	CTI	6015
'Earl Klugh'	Blue Note	BNLA 596
'Living inside your Love'	Blue Note	BNLA 667
'Finger Paintings'	Blue Note	BNLA 737

SELECTED READING

'Man of the Moment'—Earl Klugh	Herb Nolan, 'Downbeat', 24th February 1977
'Earl Klugh—Jazz/Pop Newcomer'	Robert Yelin, 'Guitar Player', July 1977

Carl Kress with George Barnes.

COURTESY GUILD GUITARS

CARL KRESS

Born—Newark, New Jersey, U.S.A.
20th October 1907

Died—Reno, Nevada, U.S.A. 10th June 1965

Carl Kress—mid-nineteen thirties.

Carl Kress first drew public attention when he was featured with the Paul Whiteman orchestra in 1926. In 1927 he recorded with two of the most outstanding musicians from the Whiteman outfit, Bix Beiderbecke and Frankie Trumbauer. During the period 1927–9 Kress was featured on more records with Miff Mole, the Dorsey Brothers, and Red Nichols amongst others.

In the early nineteen thirties Carl Kress was regarded as the leading guitarist on American radio, and recorded what are now regarded as some of the finest jazz guitar duets, firstly with Eddie Lang in 1932 and then with Dick McDonough in 1934. Carl helped found the famous 'Onyx' jazz club on

New York's 52nd Street. His fame at that time was mainly in and around the New York area, but his supremacy as one of the pioneers and masters of rhythmic chord style guitar playing was undisputed. A feature of Carl's guitar playing was his unorthodox tuning, B flat, F, C, G, A, D instead of the conventional E, A, D, G, B, C.

In the few years before his death in 1965, Kress began a new guitar duo with ace guitarist George Barnes. They made several historic recordings together which bear further testimony to the greatness of Kress. In fact it was whilst appearing with Barnes in Reno, that Kress collapsed and died at the age of 58 in 1965.

SELECTED RECORDS

'Guitar Genius in 1930's with Dick McDonough'	Jazz Archives	JA–32
'Pioneers of Jazz Guitar'	Yazoo	L1057
'Town Hall Concert' with George Barnes	United Artists	UAS 6335
'Something Tender' with Bud Freeman	United Artists	UAJ 14033
'Ten Duets for Two Guitars' with George Barnes	Music Minus One	MM04011

Nappy Lamare

NAPPY LAMARE

Born— HILTON NAPOLEON LAMARE
New Orleans, Louisiana, U.S.A.

14th June 1907

Nappy Lamare began to study the banjo at the age of 16 at the Warren Easton High School in New Orleans. For a short while he also played trumpet but he was to earn his first professional work as the banjoist with Billy Lustig's band in New Orleans' Little Club.

Lamare continued his career in New Orleans with several bands including those of Johnny Bayersdorffer, Sharkey Bonano, and Monk Hazel. Moving to New York Nappy first became nationally prominent as a guitarist when he joined the Ben Pollack band in September 1930. This band had in its personnel many of the big jazz names of the day. Bob Crosby formed his first band in 1935 with many of Pollack's musicians, including Nappy Lamare as guitarist.

In December 1942 Lamare made his home in Hollywood after joining Eddie Miller's band. During the mid-forties, he often led his own small groups but in 1948 he became once more a big band guitarist when he joined the Jimmy Dorsey outfit.

From the nineteen fifties to the present day Nappy Lamare has remained in Hollywood working successfully in a wide variety of jobs. He has not only played with dance bands, including the one led by Bob Crosby, but he has also worked on both banjo and guitar in the Hollywood film studios. He has been featured in several Walt Disney films. Despite a serious car accident in 1962 Nappy led a group successfully with Ray Bauduc on tours throughout the U.S.A. In the last few years he has led his own New Orleans style group at Disneyland.

SELECTED RECORDS

'Bob Crosby and his Band'	London	HM6 5021
'Bob Crosby and his Orchestra'	MCA	510 134
'Riverboat Dandies'	Capitol	T877

SELECTED MUSIC

'Blues for Guitar'	Five Solos by Nappy Lamare. Capitol Songs Inc.

Nappy Lamare with Bob Crosby and his band.

Eddie Lang

COURTESY C. E. H. SMITH

EDDIE LANG

Born— SALVATORE MASSARO Philadelphia, Pennsylvania, U.S.A.
1904 (possibly 1902)

Died—Philadelphia, Pennsylvania, U.S.A. 26th March 1933

Eddie Lang was the son of a south Philadelphia banjo and guitar maker. Born Salvatore Massaro he decided to choose the name of a childhood basketball hero, Eddie Lang, for his professional career. His first years of music were devoted to the violin and he attended school with jazz violinist Joe Venuti, who became Lang's closest friend until the guitarist's early death in 1933.

Venuti and Lang were to commence their professional work in Atlantic City, New Jersey. In 1924 Lang sat in with a novelty group, the 'Mound City Blue Blowers' whose record 'Arkansas Blue' became a hit. In August 1924 he decided to become a full time member of this group and this marked the start of Eddie's career as America's number one jazz guitarist. It was the influence of his strong and startling single note playing that was to mark the real beginning of the guitar as a solo instrument in jazz, rather than as part of the rhythm section. Arrangers realizing the potential of the guitar in the hands of an artist such as Lang, now included parts for the guitar in their musical arrangements. Banjo players, on hearing Lang's playing realized the limitations of their own instrument, and changed over to the guitar by the score.

The first of the historic recordings by Venuti and Lang was made in 1926—'Stringing the Blues'. During the period 1926–7 Eddie was a featured soloist with Red Nichols and his Five Pennies and as a result the virtuoso guitarist became widely known. His guitar work was much in demand by top band leaders of the day. Following his recording dates with Joe Venuti, Eddie was to record with the immortal Bix Beiderbeke. The legendary blues singer, Bessie Smith chose him as her accompanist, and under the pseudonym of 'Blind Willie Dunn' Lang recorded many superb historic guitar duets with the outstanding New Orleans guitarist Lonnie Johnson.

In 1929 Paul Whiteman finally succeeded in hiring the Venuti/Lang team as part of his orchestra. It was during his spell with Whiteman that the guitarist formed a close friendship with one of the band's vocalists Bing Crosby.

When Bing left the Whiteman organization in 1931 he was regarded as the nation's top male singer and he persuaded Lang to become his full-time accompanist. Eddie Lang had reached the top of his profession. He was regarded world-wide as 'the' jazz guitarist and could virtually demand his own fee. But, as fate would have it, Lang was to tragically die in his early twenties. Complications set in during a tonsillectomy, ending one of the most brilliant careers in jazz. Nevertheless like many other legendary jazzmen who have died in their early years Eddie Lang had made his mark in musical history. He laid down a path which most guitarists of the nineteen thirties and later were to follow.

SELECTED RECORDS

'Jazz Guitar Virtuoso'—Eddie Lang	Yazoo	1059
'Stringing the Blues'	CBS	BPG 62143
'Blue Guitars' Vol. 1	Parlophone	PMC 7019
'Blue Guitars' Vol. 2	Parlophone	PMC 7106
'Hot Strings'	Black and White	FPM1 7016
'Venuti—Lang—Rollini'	Music for Pleasure	MFP 1161

SELECTED MUSIC

'Eddie Lang's Seven Compositions'	Robbins Music Corporation
'Eddie Lang's Fingerboard Harmony'	Robbins Music Corporation

SELECTED READING

'Eddie Lang' p. 239–255	'Jazz Masters of the Twenties', Richard Hadlock—Macmillan 19
'Eddie Lang'	Richard B. Hadlock, 'Downbeat', 1st August 1963
'Eddie Lang'	Ivor Mairants, 'Guitar', February 1974

Mundell Lowe

COURTESY MELODY MAKER/PHOTO ROY BRAY

MUNDELL LOWE

Born—Laurel, Missouri, U.S.A.

21st April 1922

Mundell Lowe first studied music with his father, a church minister. He left home at the age of 14 and worked around New Orleans with a country band. After three years in various groups, including those of Abbie Brunis and Sid Devilla, Mundell arrived in Nashville in 1939. There he joined the Pee Wee King band which was featured on the 'Grand Old Opry' radio show. He stayed with this group for about six months and then continued working in various clubs in Louisiana, Florida, and Mississippi.

In 1943 Mundell joined the Army and it was whilst stationed in Louisiana that he met another army private, John Hammond, the famous jazz critic and record producer. He was promoting jam sessions and Mundell gained his first real jazz experience in these. It was Hammond that helped the young guitarist on his discharge in 1945 to gain the guitar seat with the Ray McKinley band. A two year stay with this big band gave Mundell valuable experience and in 1947 he joined pianist Mary Lou Williams for two years in New York City. He continued playing in several excellent small jazz groups including those of Red Norvo and Ellis Larkins.

In 1950 Mundell Lowe joined the NBC staff in New York for a period of 14 years. An interesting feature of his career is his interest in drama and he landed many small acting jobs, including a Broadway appearance in the play 'The Bird Cage'.

In 1965 he left for a vacation in California and this made him decide to make his home there. Actor Jackie Cooper gave him the opportunity to write music on a regular basis for the ABC—TV series 'Love on a Rooftop'. This he did with great success and he continued to write the music for many other films, television and radio shows, including 'The Iron Horse', 'Wild Wild West', and Hawaii Five-O'.

Although this involvement in the studios did not allow him to play jazz publicly, Mundell did manage to devote some time to musical education and passing the message of the art of the jazz guitar onto young players. After composing the music for the highly successful film 'Billy Jack' in 1972 Mundell recommenced to freelance on the guitar and has managed to include several jazz gigs in and around Los Angeles. In 1974 he toured Europe with singer Betty Bennett and in 1975 played with the late tenor saxophonist Richie Kamuca in many jazz clubs.

SELECTED RECORDS

'Mundell Lowe Quintet'	HMV	DLP 1084
'Mundell Lowe Quartet'	Riverside	204
'Guitar Moods'	Riverside	208
'New Music of Alec Wilder'	Riverside	219
'A Grand Night for Swinging'	Riverside	238
'TV Action Jazz'	RCA Camden	CAS 522
'Porgy and Bess'	RCA Camden	CDN 132
'Satan in High Heels'	Parker	PLP 4065
'California Guitar'	Famous Door	RL 102
'Guitar Player'	Dobre	DR 1007
'Richie'	Concord	CJ41

SELECTED MUSIC

'Guitar Impressions'	Melrose Music Corporation

SELECTED READING

'Mundell Lowe'	Jim Crockett—'Guitar Player', May/June 1972

Ivor Mairants

COURTESY JAZZ JOURNAL

IVOR MAIRANTS

Born—Rypin, Poland

18th July 1908

Ivor Mairants became a professional guitarist at the age of 20. Over the past 50 years he has gradually become regarded throughout the world as Britain's leading authority on the guitar in all its forms. Although not strictly a jazz guitarist his contribution to the promotion of the jazz guitar in Britain over the years has been enormous.

A featured member of many of Britain's leading dance bands in the nineteen thirties and forties, including those of Ambrose, Roy Fox, Lew Stone, Geraldo and Ted Heath, Ivor Mairants is still regularly featured on countless radio, television and record dates. In the last few years he has often been heard with the very popular Mantovani orchestra. Of particular importance to guitarists is the fact that Ivor has devoted so much of his time to writing music and methods for the guitar. He established a school of music in London from 1950—60 and amongst his many pupils were several players who are today some of Britain's top guitarists. Recently he has devoted a lot of his energies to developing his fine music store in the west end of London which of course specialises in the guitar.

Ivor still spends every spare moment writing for the guitar—jazz, classical and flamenco, and many of his methods and solos, old and new, are recommended for guitarists throughout the world wishing to develop their knowledge of their instrument.

SELECTED MUSIC

'New Swing Series'—6 Solos	Bosworth & Co.
'Six Evergreen Favourites'	Campbell Connoly
'Favourite Solos'	Cavendish Music Co.
'Eight Guitar Solos/Shearing Style'	Robbins Music Co.
'Latin American Favourites'	Latin American Music Co.
'Seven Swinging Standards'	Francis, Day and Hunter
'Six solos for plectrum Guitar'	Francis, Day and Hunter
'Walk with Wes'	Mills Music Co.
'Spirit of New Orleans'/'Bundle of Blues'	Hansen Music

SELECTED TUTORS—by Ivor Mairants

'Modern Chord Encyclopedia'	Francis, Day and Hunter
'Book of Daily Exercises'	Francis, Day and Hunter
'Arranging for the Guitar'	Hansen Music

Jack Marshall

COURTESY GUITAR PLAYER

JACK MARSHALL

Born—JACK WILTON MARSHALL, El Dorado, Kansas, U.S.A.
23rd November 1921

Died—Huntington Beach, California, U.S.A.
2nd September 1973

Jack Marshall began playing the ukulele at the age of 10 but it was not until he was 13 that he changed to the guitar. His first major influence was Django Reinhardt. His family moved to California in the late nineteen thirties and in 1938 Jack bought his first electric guitar having recently graduated.

Jack had the opportunity to hear and meet Oscar Moore who at that time was the featured guitarist with the Nat King Cole trio. Occasionally he would sit in for Oscar, and he also had the opportunity to play with ace pianist, Art Tatum. By the time he was 18 Jack was already playing once a week on the radio with the LAC college jazz band.

From 1940–2 Jack was an M.G.M. staff guitarist and then he spent four years in the Army. During his stay with the Army he studied both music and engineering and on leaving the Army in 1946 he decided to continue his engineering studies at the University of South California, and played jazz for pleasure. He graduated in engineering but by that time his love for music had become so great that he decided to become a full time professional musician. In 1950 he studied orchestration and

harmony in depth with the famed Albert Harris. At the same time he was working once more in the M.G.M. studios. He also took up the classical guitar but decided that his main love was writing. Amongst his musical works are over 300 television and film works, as well as a guitar concerto for his cousin, the classical guitarist Christopher Parkening.

Jack Marshall's love for the guitar was enormous and in 1967 it was he that persuaded the owners of the Dontés' night club in Burbank, Los Angeles to start a weekly guitar night. These evenings became historic as they featured and were attended by the cream of America's jazz guitarists.

At the height of his career Jack Marshall tragically collapsed and died of a heart attack in September 1973. To honour his name, the fraternity of guitarists and musicians in the Los Angeles area, put on a special show at Dontés to raise money to establish a scholarship in his name. This they did with great success and today young guitarists, who show ability, are able to use the Marshall Scholarship at the University of Southern California to develop their talents further.

SELECTED RECORDS

'Sounds Unheard Of'	Contemporary	LAC 539
'Sounds'	Capitol	ST 2610
'18th Century Jazz'	Capitol	T 1108
'Soundsville'	Capitol	T 1194

SELECTED MUSIC

'West Coast Guitar'	Leeds Music
'Bossa Nova Guitar'	MCA Music
'20 Popular Introductions and Endings'	MCA Music
'Guitar Get Together' Vols. 1 and 2	MCA Music

SELECTED READING

'Jack Marshall'	Morgan Hope—'Guitar Player', October 1972
'Jack Marshal—A Tribute'	Leonard Feather—'Guitar Player', March 1974

Pat Martino

PAT MARTINO

Born—PAT AZZARA, Philadelphia, Pennsylvania

25th August 1944

Pat Martino was exposed to the guitar at a very early age as his father was a singer who also played the guitar His father had a collection of records including many by his favourite guitarists Eddie Lang, Django Reinhardt, and Johnny Smith.

Pat was first influenced by a local guitarist called Dennis Sandhole and after only four years on the instrument he was playing professionally with various Rhythm and Blues bands, including those of Willis Jackson and Brother Jack McDuff.

Martino found that Rhythm and Blues did not have the depth and scope for his obvious musical talent. He decided to further his musical studies and at the same time earn a living with some studio work. Pat worked as a sideman with several jazz groups including that of John Handy and in 1967 made his first record as leader of his own group. Within one year his exceptional technique and exciting improvisations brought great admiration from critics and guitarists alike. Since then Pat has continued to record records as leader and still seems to be searching for his own musical ideal. He continues to experiment and investigate the full spectrum of modern music. At first Pat had a great love of the Wes Montgomery style, this led into the study of Eastern music, and of recent he has headed a jazz/rock band. Synthesizers and free form are now all a part of Martino's unique playing, and there seems no doubt that he will play a great part in the evolution of the jazz guitar in the next few years.

SELECTED RECORDS

'Hombre'	Prestige	7513
'Strings'	Prestige	7547
'The Visit'	Cobblestone	9015
'Live'	Muse	5026
'East'	Prestige	7562
'Desperado'	Prestige	7795
'Baiyina'	Prestige	7589
'Exit'	Muse	5075
'We'll be Together Again'	Muse	5090
'Consciousness'	Muse	5039
'Joyous Lake'	Warner Bros.	BS2977

SELECTED READING

'Pat Martino—Musician First'	'Downbeat', 6th February 1969
'Pat Martino'	Robert Yelin, 'Guitar Player', September 1973
'Lightning Bug in Eclectic Jar'	Kent Hazen, 'Downbeat', 9th October 1975
'Pat Martino'	Vic Trigger, 'Guitar Player', June 1977

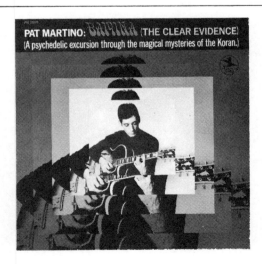

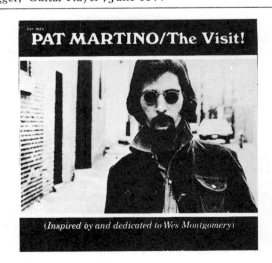

CARMEN MASTREN

Born— CARMEN NICHOLAS MASTREN
Cohoes, New York, U.S.A.

6th October 1913

Carmen Mastren

Carmen Mastren originally began his musical career on the banjo and violin, but changed to the guitar in 1931. Coming from a musical family, all his four brothers were musicians, Carmen's first major break was when he joined Wingy Manone in 1935 in New York City, and then later from 1936—40 with the Tommy Dorsey Band, where his distinctive acoustic guitar breaks and fill-ins were often featured. In 1941 he played with Joe Marsala and Ernie Holst.

Carmen worked as a member of the NBC staff until 1943 when he was drafted into the Army and he was fortunate to be given the guitar seat in Glenn Miller's Air Force band. On leaving the Army in 1946 Mastren returned to the studios in New York.

Since that time Carmen Mastren, a direct link to the guitar styles of Eddie Lang and Dick McDonough, has had little connection with jazz. From 1953—70 he was permanently with the NBC and since that time had occupied his time freelancing, and writing jingles for television adverts.

SELECTED RECORDS

'Adrian Rollini and Friends'	Black and White	FPM1—7010
'Glenn Miller's Uptown Hall Gang'	Esquire	302
'Bechet Original Sessions 1940'	Jazz Anthology	30JA—5109
'Bechet/Spanier Quartet'	Ember	SE 8023

Carmen Mastren with the American Air Force band.

COURTESY ESQUIRE RECORDS

DICK McDONOUGH

Born— RICHARD McDONOUGH
1904

Died—New York City 25th May 1938

Dick McDonough

Dick McDonough's recordings, which are now once more available, make us realize what a loss to the jazz world his early death was.

McDonough, like many guitarists of the nineteen thirties was originally a banjoist. Following the trends set by Eddie Lang and Lonnie Johnson he changed to guitar and developed a style of playing that set unsurpassed standards for guitarists until the arrival of the electric guitar.

His virtuosity on the instrument and musical talents ensured that he was one of the busiest musicians in New York City. McDonough not only led his own radio and recording band but he was a featured soloist on literally hundreds of recordings with other bands such as those of Red Nichols and the Dorsey Brothers. In the early nineteen thirties he made some historic guitar duo records with Carl Kress but this partnership came to an abrupt end when the thirty-four-year-old guitarist collapsed in the NBC studios in New York. Despite an emergency operation he died a little later in hospital on 25th May 1938.

SELECTED RECORDS

'Dick McDonough and Carl Kress'	Jazz Archives	JA 32
'Pioneers of Jazz Guitar'	Yazoo	L—1057
'Fifty Years of Jazz Guitar'	Columbia	33566

SELECTED READING
'Dick McDonough' Ivor Mairants, 'Guitar', March 1974

COURTESY CBS RECORDS

John McLaughlin

JOHN McLAUGHLIN

Born—Kirk Sandell, near Doncaster, Yorkshire, England

4th January 1942

McLaughlin was born into a musical family, his mother was a violinist, and all his three brothers were musicians. Music, mainly classical, was always in his background, but it was not until he was nine that he was to first take a few piano lessons. This continued for three years until a guitar belonging to one of his brothers ended up in his hands. At the age of 12 his deep love for the guitar first came to fruit via the blues styles of Big Bill Broonzy, Muddy Waters, and Leadbelly.

At the age of 14 John was exposed to the guitar sounds of Django Reinhardt and then a little later those of Tal Farlow, Jim Hall and Barney Kessel. This redirected his musical development. He led his own band at school and in the next few years his study of music included the jazz sounds of Miles Davis and John Coltrane, as well as the classical masters Bartok and Debussy, all of which were to help McLaughlin develop his own very individual style.

For six years he gained important experience playing in all types of groups, mainstream to avant garde, and also Rhythm and Blues. His first major job was with the Graham Bond organization which he joined at the age of 21. Other musicians in this group included Jack Bruce and Ginger Baker. John also played with artists such as Georgie Fame and Brian Auger. During his years living in London John was continuously experimenting with many of the electric guitar concepts that are now regarded as an everyday thing in a jazz/rock guitarist's playing.

It was in 1968 that McLaughlin decided to make the break from Britain and he left for the United States where his first break was with 'Lifetime' the group led by Tony Williams. Williams was a great admirer of McLaughlin's original and vigorous style, as was trumpeter Miles Davis who was later to record several times with the young British guitarist.

The next great turning point came when McLaughlin met the guru, Sri Chinmoy. This meeting changed John's attitude to life and also gave him the motivation to form his own group and play a new style of music which was greatly influenced by the East. The outcome was the now famed 'Mahavishnu Orchestra' in which his guitar playing, usually on a specially built twin neck guitar, was the driving force. For many the exotic sounds and rhythms of this group were the best thing to happen to both jazz and rock music for a long time.

Since 1975 McLaughlin's love for the East and its way of life has even more greatly influenced his playing. His group 'Shakti' made up of Indian instrumentalists and vocalists caused almost as big a sensation as the original Mahavishnu orchestra. In this group John plays a specially built acoustic Gibson guitar which incorporates 'drones', normally found on Indian instruments.

His current venture is reported to be the formation of new Mahavishnu band with legendary drummer Billy Cobham.

SELECTED RECORDS

'Bitches Brew' with Miles Davis	Columbia	GP 26
'Extrapolation'	Polydor	231—018
'My Goals Beyond'	Douglas	2 30766
'Shakti—Natural Elements'	CBS	82329
'John McLaughlin Electric Guitarist'	CBS	82702

SELECTED READING

'The Magic of Mahavishnu'	Mike Bourne, 'Downbeat', 8th June 1972
'Extending Beyond Mahavishnu'	Burt Korall, 'Downbeat' 7th June 1973
'Mahavishnu's Apocalypse'	Jim Schaffer, 'Downbeat', 16th June 1974
'McLaughlin—Un Anglais Aux Dents Longues'	'Jazz Magazine', July 1970
'John McLaughlin'	Vic Trigger—'Guitar Player', December 1972
'My Life and the Guitar'	Steve Rosen—'Guitar Player', February 1975
'John McLaughlin'	Tony Jasper—'Guitar', March 1975

Mahavishnu Orchestra.

Shakti

John McLaughlin with his famous twin neck guitar.

COURTESY CBS RECORDS

PAT METHENY

Born—Lee Summit, Missouri, U.S.A.

12th August 1954

Pat Metheny

Pat Metheny is one of the new generation of jazz/rock guitarists who are making a great impression on this particular movement in jazz of the nineteen seventies.

Pat started on the guitar at the age of 14 and was influenced by trumpeter Miles Davis as well as guitarist Wes Montgomery. Whilst he was still at high school in Kansas City, Metheny played in various jazz groups. He won a 'Downbeat' magazine scholarship to a stage band camp. Here he met Atilla Zoller who invited him to New York to see and hear the New York jazz scene at first hand. This visit made Pat decide that he wanted to be a jazz musician.

After leaving school Pat went to the University of Miami where he taught guitar for a year, as well as doing club and studio work. His first major break came when he met vibist Gary Burton in Wichita, Kansas. The brilliant vibes player was greatly impressed by Pat's guitar style and helped him gain a teaching post at Boston's Berklee College of Music, and also to record for the German company ECM.

Since that time Pat has taught and played in both Boston and New York, his reputation on the guitar steadily gaining stature.

SELECTED RECORDS

'Bright Size Life'—Pat Metheny Trio	ECM	1073
'Water Colours'—Pat Metheny Trio	ECM	1097
'Pat Metheny Group'	ECM	1114

SELECTED READING

'Gary Burtons Star Guitarists'	Michael A. Meltzer, 'Guitar Player', March 1976
'Pat Metheny'	Les Tomkins, 'Crescendo', May 1978

Wes Montgomery

COURTESY JAZZ JOURNAL/PHOTO ROY MATHERS

WES MONTGOMERY

Born— JOHN LESLIE MONTGOMERY
Indianapolis, Indiana, U.S.A. 6th March 1925

Died—Indianapolis, Indiana, U.S.A. 15th June 1968

Unlike most of the world's finest jazz guitarists, past or present John Leslie 'Wes' Montgomery started to play the guitar very late in life. At the age of 19 in 1942, inspired by the records of Charlie Christian, he began to play the guitar. He developed a technique of single notes, octaves and chords which was so facile that many times what he played, previous to his emergence on the scene, would have thought to have been technically impossible. Wes used his thumb instead of pick on the right hand and so produced a unique and instantly recognizable sound. His talent was soon much in demand. After only six months of playing the guitar he was hired by a local band to play nothing but Charlie Christian's solos note for note. Not being able to read music his magnificent musical ear showed its strength at this early time and helped his rapid progress. Together with brothers, Monk on bass, and Buddy on piano, the Montgomery brothers soon became a vital part of the Indianapolis jazz scene, although unknown beyond there.

Until 1959 Wes remained virtually unknown outside Indianapolis, even though he spent two years on the road with the renowned Lionel Hampton Band. During this time his band mates had nicknamed him 'Rev' Montgomery because he was a teetotaller.

Wes was a devoted family man and having six children, the road life that was the lot of most jazz musicians did not appeal to him. Nevertheless his thirst to play gave him a most arduous working day. From 7.00 a.m. to 3.00 p.m. he would work in a local radio factory. After a brief rest he would play jazz in the nearby Turf Bar from 9.00 p.m.—2.00 a.m. and then more jazz in another club, the Missile Room, from 2.30 a.m. to 5.00 a.m.

In true storybook style it was a chance visit by the world famous jazz saxophonist Cannonball Adderley on a one night stand to Indianapolis that was to reveal to the world the colossal talent of Wes Montgomery. Cannonball heard Wes in the Missile Room, and was so taken aback by the brilliance of Wes's playing that he immediately rang Orrin Keepnews the head of the then very successful 'Riverside' jazz recording company. He urged him to sign up Montgomery without delay. Keepnew was a bit sceptical of Adderly's adulation but coincidentally he noticed an article by the renowned composer—musician—critic Gunther Schuller in a current issue of the magazine 'The Jazz Review'. In this article entitled 'The Indiana Renaissance' Schuller wrote 'The thing that it is most easy to say about Wes Montgomery is that he is an extraordinary spectacular guitarist. Listening to his solos is like teetering continually on the edge of a brink. His playing at its peak becomes unbearably exciting to the point where one feels unable to muster sufficient physical endurance to outlast it.'

Within a few days Keepnew was listening to Wes at the Turf Bar and the Missile Room and needless to say Wes was quickly signed up for Riverside. His first record was waxed in New York on 5th and 6th October 1959 with his trio from Indianapolis, consisting of Melvin Rhyne—organ, and Paul Parker—drums. From then on success followed success. Shortly after January 1960 Wes made probably his finest record, and one of the finest jazz records ever made. 'The Incredible Jazz Guitar of Wes Montgomery.' In the following eight years Wes was to become the most popular and most recorded of jazz guitarists of the sixties. His records constantly topped the best selling charts. Many of his records were made with big orchestras in a commercial vain. Yet he still retained his distinctive jazz style which appealed to both jazz lovers and the general public alike.

He received awards from 'Downbeat', 'Billboard' and 'Playboy' as guitarist and Jazzman of the Year. He received the 'Grammy' award for the 'Best Instrumental Jazz Performance of 1967' and he was profiled in such magazines as 'Time' and 'Newsweek', rare recognition for a jazz artist. He toured the world as his reputation became known world-wide, displaying his genius in city after city, including London where he played at Ronnie Scott's Club.

At the height of his career in the summer of 1968, Wes collapsed and died at the age of 44. A tragic and irreplaceable loss to the whole musical world.

SELECTED RECORDS

'The Trio'	Riverside	1156
'Boss Guitar'	Riverside	9459
'Moving Along'	Riverside	9342
'Vibratin''	Riverside	9499
'So Much Guitar'	Riverside	9382
'Round Midnight'	Riverside	RS 3014
'Fusion'	Riverside	9472
'Guitar On the Go'	Riverside	9494
'The Incredible Jazz Guitar of Wes Montgomery'	Riverside	RLP 12—320
'Full House'	Riverside	RLP 9434
'California Dreaming'	Verve	SVLP 9162
'Willow Weep for Me'	Verve	SVLP 9238
'Going out of my Head'	Verve	SVLP 9126
'Tequila'	Verve	VLP 9143
'Movin' Wes'	Verve	VLP 9092
'Bumpin''	Verve	V6 8625
'Down here on the Ground'	A & M	AMLS 3006
'A Day in the Life'	A & M	AML 2001

SELECTED MUSIC

'Wes Montgomery Jazz Guitar Method'	Robbins Music Corp.
'Wes Montgomery Jazz Guitar Solos'	Almo Music Corp.

SELECTED READING

'Wes Montgomery'	Ralph J. Gleason—'Downbeat', 20th July 1961
'Wes Montgomery — Guitarists' Problems with Organs'	Ira Gitler, 'Downbeat', July 1964
'Thumbs Up'	Bill Quinn—'Downbeat', 27th June 1968
'Wes Montgomery—1925—68'	Ralph J. Gleason, 'Guitar Player', July/August 1973

Wes Montgomery

COURTESY GUITAR/PHOTO GEORGE CLINTON

OSCAR MOORE

Born– OSCAR FRED MOORE
Austin, Texas, U.S.A.

25th December 1916

Oscar Moore with the Three Blazers

COURTESY JAZZ JOURNAL

Oscar Moore first played the guitar professionally in 1934 at the age of 18 with his brother Johnny Moore. Three years later he achieved international fame when he joined the Nat King Cole Trio, a position he was to hold for 10 years.

The records made with King Cole from 1937 are evidence of the high standard of Moore's guitar work. There is no doubt that his playing ability and importance in jazz have been under-rated and this probably due to his emergence on the jazz scene coinciding with that of Charlie Christian. Nevertheless Oscar Moore was harmonically well ahead of his time in jazz and he won many jazz polls both in 'Downbeat' and 'Metronome' magazines, from the years 1945—9.

In 1949 Oscar left King Cole's trio to settle in Los Angeles where he rejoined his brother Jimmy in a group called 'The Three Blazers'. He has remained on the West Coast ever since that time making some 'pop' records and also the occasional jazz record.

SELECTED RECORDS

'Nat King Cole Trio'	DJM Records	DJS LM 2029
'Nat King Cole Trio'	Music for Pleasure	MFP 1129
'Oscar Moore Trio'	Vedette	VDS 213
'Fabulous Guitar'	Parker	830

SELECTED MUSIC

'Guitaristics'—Oscar Moore Guitar Solos	Leeds Music Corp.

Mary Osborne

COURTESY GUITAR PLAYER

MARY OSBORNE

Born—Minot, Bismark, North Dakota, U.S.A.

17th July 1921

Mary Osborne holds the distinction of being the only female jazz guitarist to be listed in this book. Mary had the fortune to come from a strong musical background, her parents both played the guitar, whilst her father also led his own band.

At the age of four Mary could already strum the ukulele and at school she was making progress on the violin. But it was at the age of nine that she took up the guitar and it quickly wove its spell on Mary. Throughout her teens Mary sang and played jazz guitar in various clubs in the Bismark area. At that time her influences were Eddie Lang, Django Reinhardt and Dick McDonough, but on the advice of her friends she went to hear Charlie Christian playing with the Al Trent Sextet. Hearing the fantastic guitar sound of Christian brought a sudden change to Mary's approach to the guitar and jazz. She immediately went out and bought an electric guitar fitted with a bar pickup. Mary was fortunate to develop a friendship with Christian and this was a further influence on her style.

Not too long after, Mary joined the Winifred McDonald trio and toured various states with the group, finally ending up in New York City. Here the group split up, but because of her fine ability on the guitar Mary earned many radio and recording jobs. She found herself much in demand in the 52nd Street jazz clubs, earning a place in

pianist Mary Lou Williams trio and then later the guitar seat in the Dick Stabile band. Mary continued to travel ending up in Chicago where she was kept busy both with radio work and in jazz clubs. Whilst in Chicago in 1944 she was heard by Leonard Feather who later put her on in concert in New Orleans. This was to gain her national recognition amongst jazz fans. Her next stop was to be Philadelphia where she appeared in concert with the legendary saxophonist Coleman Hawkins.

In 1946 Mary married trumpeter Ralph Scaffidi and they decided to settle in New York City where Mary, with her own trio, played in jazz spots like 'Kelly's Stables'. Her fame became widely known and among the visitors to the clubs who came to hear her play was Django Reinhardt. The trio broke up in 1949 and Mary went freelance, becoming one of the busiest guitarists around until 1962, playing and recording with many of the top studio bands. Her love for the guitar has never dwindled and for a period of five years from 1962 she also studied the classical guitar with Albert Valdes Blain in New York.

In 1968 the Scaffidis' moved to California with their three children. Here Mary still maintains an active musical life, leading her own quartet in various night spots, as well as teaching and playing the classical guitar.

SELECTED RECORDS'

'Esquire All-American Jazz'	Vintage	LPV544
'A Girl and her Guitar'	Warwick	2004

SELECTED READING

'Mary Osborne'	Leonard Ferris—'Guitar Player', February 1974

REMO PALMIER

Born— REMO PALMIERI
New York City, U.S.A.

29th March 1923

Remo Palmier

COURTESY REMO PALMIER/PHOTO CHRIS CASCONE

Palmier originally played the guitar to pay for his art studies, as he hoped to be a professional artist. His first professional job as a musician was with the Nat Jaffe trio in 1942. Remo soon developed a reputation as one of the most advanced of the East coast guitarists playing in a Charlie Christian influenced style. In 1943 he played with Coleman Hawkins and later in 1944 with Red Norvo. Leading his own group, Remo also backed singer Billie Holliday in jazz clubs on 52nd Street.

In 1944 he played behind Mildred Bailey on a CBS radio series and at the same time was regularly featured with the Phil Moore orchestra at the 'Cafe Society'. In 1945 Remo recorded several times with both Dizzy Gillespie and Barney Bigard. That same year he joined the CBS in New York and worked mainly on the very popular Arthur Godfrey show. Here he remained, exiled from jazz, playing in the NBC studios until 1972.

Since 1972 Palmier has made a modest return to the jazz scene, freelancing for a period with his own quartet at various clubs with artists such as pianist Hank Jones and trumpeter Bobby Hackett. In 1974 he joined the Benny Goodman orchestra for several major jazz concerts. He has recently recorded with Herb Ellis for the Concord label.

SELECTED RECORDS

'Esquire All American Hot Jazz'	Vintage	LPV 544
'Teddy Wilson Sextet'	Everest	FS 263
'The Everlasting Teddy Wilson'	Vernon	505
'Wildflower'	Concord	CJ 56

BLUE GUITARS
Eddie Lang & Lonnie Johnson

I'LL NEVER BE THE SAME
APRIL KISSES
PRELUDE (IN C SHARP MINOR)
THE MELODY MAN'S DREAM
PERFECT
CHURCH ST. SOBBIN' BLUES
THERE'LL BE SOME CHANGES MADE
JEANNINE (I DREAM OF LILAC TIME)
TWO TONE STOMP
GUITAR BLUES
BULL FROG MOAN
A HANDFUL OF RIFFS
WORK OX BLUES*
THE RISIN' SUN*
JET BLACK BLUES**
BLUE BLOOD BLUES**
*with TEXAS ALEXANDER
**BLIND WILLIE DUNN'S GIN BOTTLE FOUR

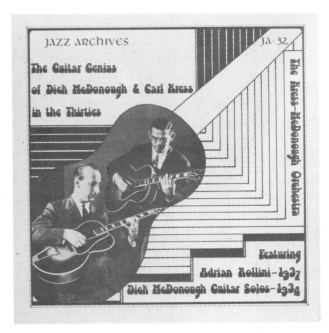

JAZZ ARCHIVES   JA-32

The Guitar Genius
of Dick McDonough & Carl Kress
in the Thirties

The Kress-McDonough Orchestra

Featuring
Adrian Rollini — 1937
Dick McDonough Guitar Solos — 1934

Take Your Pick
GUITAR DUETS

Johnny **Pisano**   Billy **Bean**

MOOD *jazz* IN HI-FI

TOWN HALL CONCERT • GEORGE BARNES'S CARL KRESS • UNITED ARTISTS UAL 3335

george **BARNES** / town hall **CONCERT**
carl **KRESS**

LOVE IS JUST AROUND THE CORNER • RIDIN' MY TIME •
SOMETHING TENDER • PRAISE BE! • THREE LITTLE WORDS •
SOMEONE TO WATCH OVER ME • DUET FOR THREE GUITARS •
BERNIE'S TUNE • GOLDEN RETRIEVER PUPPY • SNOWFALL •
MOUNTAIN GREENERY • LIEBESFREUD • A FOGGY DAY • • •

Barney Kessel *Poor Butterfly* Herb Ellis

LET YOUR FINGERS DO THE WALKING   6000

MARTY GROSZ   WAYNE WRIGHT

ACOUSTIC GUITAR DUETS

A selection of fine jazz guitar duets on record from the nineteen-twenties to the present day.

COURTESY PABLO RECORDS

Joe Pass

JOE PASS

Born—JOSEPH ANTHONY JACOBI PASSALAQUA
New Brunswick, New Jersey, U.S.A.

13th January 1929

Joe Pass, the oldest of four children, spent his youth in the Italian area of Johnstown, Pennsylvania. His father Mariano Passalaqua was a steel mill worker. Joe started playing the guitar at the age of nine and received his first lessons from friends of his father. With great encouragement from his father, Joe took weekly lessons and spent most of his spare time practising and playing. By the time he was fourteen Joe was already working with local bands for weddings and dances.

He fell in love with the sounds of Be Bop as he reached his twenties and Joe moved to New York where he could hear the finest jazz musicians of the day. Unfortunately whilst soaking up the music scene in New York in 1949 he became addicted to drugs. For 12 years, until 1960, his brilliance was stifled under the influence of drugs. He was in fact arrested several times and as a result had to serve time for his addiction.

In 1960 Joe made the wise decision to enter Synanon, which was then a special centre for the rehabilitation of musicians who were addicted to drugs. He stayed there for three years, was totally cured of the habit and he was able to set himself on a straight course for his musical career. Whilst residing at Synanon he made a record with a group made up of other musicians who were residents at the hospital. It was called 'Sounds of Synanon' and on hearing it the jazz critics raved about Joe's guitar playing. He soon left Synanon, fully cured, and started working in and around Los Angeles with many top jazz names.

In 1968 he joined the studios for a period of five years before being persuaded to join Norman Granz's world jazz concert tours. Granz recognized Pass's genius and signed him up for his Pablo recording company.

The last four years have seen a meteoric rise to fame for Joe Pass under the guidance of promoter Norman Granz. He is often titled the 'Virtuoso of the Jazz Guitar' and also the 'Art Tatum of the Guitar'. Certainly his unique style of solo playing can be linked to the virtuoso piano style of the late Art Tatum. With the Pablo label Joe Pass not only records solo but plays with many different line-ups. In all areas of guitar playing Joe now shows that he is one of the few all time greats of the jazz guitar.

SELECTED RECORDS

'Sounds of Synanon'	Fontana	688139
'A Sign of the Times'	World Pacific	WP 1844
'Catch Me'	Fontana	688 137 ZL
'For Django'	Fontana	688 146 ZL
'Intercontinental'	MPS CRM	738
'Take Love Easy' with Ella Fitzgerald	Pablo	2310 702
'Duke Ellington's Big 4'	Pablo	2310 703
'Portrait of the Duke'	Pablo	2310 716
'Dizzy Gillespie's Big 4'	Pablo	2310 719
'Two for the Road' with Herb Ellis	Pablo	2310 714
'Seven come Eleven' with Herb Ellis	Concord	CJ2
'Jazz Concord' with Herb Ellis	Concord	CJ1
'The Big 3'	Pablo	2310 757
'Fitzgerald and Pass Again'	Pablo	2310 772
'Virtuoso'	Pablo	2310 708
'At Montreux 75'	Pablo	2310 752
'A Salle Pleyel'	Pablo	2657 015
'Porgy and Bess'	Pablo	2310 779
'Virtuoso 2'	Pablo	2310 788
'At Montreux 77'	Pablo	2308 212
'Guitar Interludes'	Discovery	DS—776
'Virtuoso 3'	Pablo	2310—805

SELECTED MUSIC
*'Joe Pass Guitar Style'   Gwyn Publishing Co.
 'Joe Pass Solos'   Gwyn Publishing Co.
 'Joe Pass Guitar Chords'   Gwyn Publishing Co.
 Joe Pass Chord Solos'   Gwyn Publishing Co.
*'Joe Pass Jazz Duets'   Gwyn Publishing Co.
 'Joe Pass Guitar Method'   Theodore Presser Co.

*Cassettes by Joe Pass available of this music.

SELECTED READING
'Joe Pass—Building a New Life'   John Tynan, 'Downbeat', 1st August 1963
'Joe Pass—Life on the Far Side of the Hour Glass'   Lee Underwood, 'Downbeat', 13th March 1975
'Joe Pass—Jazz Virtuoso'   John Sievert, 'Guitar Player', April 1976
'Joe Pass'   George Clinton, 'Guitar', June 1974
'Joe Pass Interview'   Burnett James, 'Jazz Journal' May 1976
'Joe Pass Discography'   Chris Sheridan, 'Jazz Journal' May/June 1976
'Joe Pass'   Lee Underwood, 'Downbeat', 1978

Joe Pass

COURTESY PABLO RECORDS

Joe Pass

COURTESY PABLO RECORDS

JAZZ DUETS

By JOE PASS and HERB ELLIS

GWYN PUBLISHING COMPANY
P. O. Box 5900
SHERMAN OAKS, CALIFORNIA 91413

$4.25

JAZZ GUITAR SOLOS

By JOE PASS

Les Paul

COURTESY GUITAR/PHOTO GEORGE CLINTON

LES PAUL

Born—LESTER WILLIAM POLFUS
Waukesha, Wisconsin, U.S.A.

9th June 1916

Les Paul is today one of the most well known names amongst the millions of guitarists throughout the world. This is by virtue of the many solid body electric guitars designed by Les and made by the Gibson company in the U.S.A., and also by his development of multi-track recording. Probably not many of these guitarists realize that Les Paul is also an outstanding guitarist who won many jazz polls in the late forties.

Les Paul fell in love with the guitar at an early age. He was self taught both on the guitar and the harmonica, which he played mounted on a harness so that he could play both instruments simultaneously. His first professional work was really as a 'one man band', playing for tips at roadside restaurants. He used to call himself 'Rhubarb Red' and his reputation soon earned him some local radio broadcasts, particularly when he teamed up with Joe Wolverton whose stage name was 'Singing Joe'.

In the early nineteen thirties he left for Chicago where his obvious natural talent earned him many jobs in the various local radio stations. His dual ability of being able to play country and western under the name of 'Rhubarb Red' and jazz as Les Paul ensured that he was kept very busy. It is interesting to note that in a 1934 'Gibson Guitar' catalogue he is shown as a Gibson guitar user, but under the name of 'Rhubarb Red'. After five years in Chicago Les moved to New York where he had his own trio in which he played electric guitar. This trio appeared with Fred Waring and his Pennsylvanians. By the mid-forties he was regarded as one of America's foremost jazz guitarists, obviously greatly influenced by Django Reinhardt, and he was chosen to appear in Norman Granz's 'Jazz at the Philharmonic'.

Besides the obvious importance of his exceptional development of the solid electric guitar, Les Paul is also renowned for his brilliant multi-track guitar recordings with singer Mary Ford. His first experiments into this field began as early as 1937, but it was not until 1946, under the persuasion of the late Bing Crosby, that Les built his own studio to develop and perfect his multi-track recording techniques. Multi-track recording is part and parcel of the music scene today but it was in Les's home studio that he made the first historic multi-track recordings, 'Lover' and 'Brazil'. When these records were released they received unprecedented commercial success.

Not long after the release of the first Les Paul multi-track records Les was involved in a serious car accident in which he almost lost his right arm. Miraculously his arm was saved by an astute doctor who was a Les Paul fan and immediately recognized the guitarist. With the use of a metal plate the doctor was able to set the right arm in such a way that Les could play the guitar.

After his release from hospital, because of his disability, Les was anxious to further develop his experiments with the solid body guitar, which he had begun in the late nineteen thirties. He realized the compactness of the solid guitar would now suit his damaged right arm better than the conventional hollow body guitars.

In 1949 he met and married singer Colleen Summers (Mary Ford) and they were to make many very successful multi-track vocal and guitar hits together. Over the years Les became more and more convinced that there was a demand for a solid guitar and by the early nineteen fifties he had persuaded the Gibson company to produce the first Les Paul solid guitars. At first these only received a cool reception. It was not until the nineteen sixties, with the arrival of Rock and Roll, that the solid guitar suddenly became a runaway success, and now the Les Paul solid guitar has become probably the most popular, and the most copied guitar the world has known.

Today, Les Paul resides at his home in Mahwah, New Jersey, and after a ten year break from professional work he now tours the U.S.A. playing and recording with a variety of artists. He is without doubt one of the most popular figures in the music industry, his very individual guitar style and sound still instantly recognisable.

SELECTED RECORDS

'Jazz at the Philharmonic'	Verve	2610 020
'Les Paul Trio'	Tops	1602
'Bye Bye Blues'	Capitol	356
'The Hit Makers'	Capitol	416
'Time to Dream'	Capitol	862
'Les Paul—Now'	Decca	PFS 4138
'Chester and Lester' (with Chet Atkins)	RCA	APL1—1167

SELECTED MUSIC

'The Guitar Magic of Les Paul'	Leeds Music Corp.

SELECTED READING

'The Best Advice I Ever Had'	Les Paul, 'Readers Digest', July 1957
'Les Paul'	'Guitar Player', February 1970
'The Original Les Paul'	Ivor Mairants, 'Guitar', February 1975
'Les Paul—Guitar Talking'	Ralph Denyer, 'Guitar', November 1975
'Les Paul'	Ivor Mairants, 'Guitar', December 1975
'Les Paul—Father of the Rock Guitar'	Chris Charlesworth, 'Melody Maker', 20th September 1975
'Les Paul'	Jon Sievert, 'Guitar Player', December 1977

Les Paul with Django Reinhardt.

COURTESY MELODY MAKER/PHOTO JEAN PIERRE LELOIR

JOHN PISANO

Born—New York City, U.S.A.

6th February 1931

John Pisano

COURTESY GUITAR PLAYER

Although John Pisano did not start playing the guitar until he was 14 he did have a good musical background. He had studied the piano at the age of 10 and his father was an amateur guitarist. Whilst he was in the U.S.A. Air Force from 1952–5 he joined the Air Force band. It was then that he decided to make music his career.

After he left the forces John joined the famed Chico Hamilton quintet on the recommendation of flautist Paul Horn. Whilst touring with Hamilton, Pisano decided to settle in Los Angeles where in 1958 he recorded some outstanding duets with fellow guitarist Billy Bean.

For a period of two years he furthered his musical studies at a local city college and at the same time was chosen to back singer Peggy Lee. This was to prove to be a long and successful association. In the mid-nineteen sixties John's talents were brought to the attention of trumpeter Herb Alpert, leader of the popular 'Tijuana Brass'. Alpert signed him up with the group for four years and Pisano toured the world with this very popular band. John was also associated during the same period with composer/songwriter Burt Bacharach as well as the brilliant South American group 'Brazil 66' led by pianist Sergio Mendes.

In recent times John has been featured with guitarists Lee Ritenour and Tony Rizzi, once more backing Peggy Lee, and also writing music. He spends most of his time in and around Los Angeles where his guitar virtuosity is constantly in demand.

SELECTED RECORDS

'Chico Hamilton Quintet'	Pacific Jazz	1225
'Making It' duo with Billie Bean	Decca	9206
'Take Your Pick' duo with Billie Bean	Decca	9212
'Fred Katz and his Jammers'	Decca	79217

SELECTED READING

'John Pisano'	Frankie R. Nemko, 'Guitar Player', November 1974

BUCKY PIZZARELLI

Born— JOHN PIZZARELLI
Paterson, New Jersey, U.S.A.

9th January 1926

Bucky was introduced to the guitar, at the age of nine, by two uncles who were both guitarists. His first professional work was as a rhythm guitarist in local dance bands in 1941. By the time he was 17 he had joined the popular dance band led by Vaughan Monroe. He toured with this outfit for about three months and then Bucky found himself drafted into the Army. After he left the forces the young guitarist rejoined the Monroe band and he spent the next five years with them.

In 1952 he decided to resettle in his home town of Paterson, New Jersey where he played in a local trio led by Joe Mooney. Bucky was then offered a job by the NBC as staff guitarist for a five day a week television show. He took this position and found he was also able to fit in club and recording work, as well as playing with diverse groups including the Les Elgart band.

From 1955 to 1957 Bucky spent a lot of time on the road with a group called 'The Three Sins'. It was then that he met the brilliant guitarist George Barnes. They found that their musical ideas 'clicked' and Bucky backed Barnes on many occasions. He then decided to go back into the lucrative studio and recording work, and gained vast experience, playing with most of the top East Coast studio guitarists including Al Caiola, Tony Mottola and Mundell Lowe.

By chance in 1967 Bucky heard George Van Eps playing his seven string guitar in a New York club, and fascinated by the extra harmonies gained with the extra string Bucky was determined to master the seven stringed instrument. Whilst developing his technique on this guitar Bucky renewed his association with George Barnes, whose long time partner Carl Kress had recently died. Together they formed a new and exciting guitar duo. They found that once more they had a great rapport for each others type of music and together they played many concerts and made several excellent recordings.

In 1970 Bucky decided to accept an offer to join the Benny Goodman orchestra and except for a break during 1971 stayed with that prestigious outfit until 1974. Since then Bucky spends a lot of his time recording with various artists and also giving solo recitals in jazz clubs and concerts, on the seven string guitar, throughout the U.S.A.

SELECTED RECORDS

'Jazz minus many Men'	Savoy	MG 12158
'Nightwings'	Flying Dutchman	BDL 1—1120
'Green Guitar Blues'	Monmouth	MES 7047
'Bucky Plays Bix and Kress'	Monmouth	MES 7066
'Guitars—Pure and Honest'	A & R Records	7100—077
'Town Hall Concert'	CBS	S67275
'A Flower for all Seasons'	Choice	CRS 1002
'Buck and Bud'	Flying Dutchman	BDL 1—1378
'Sliding By' with Joe Venuti	Sonet	SNTF 734
'Bucky's Bunch'	Monmouth	MES 7082

SELECTED MUSIC

'A Touch of Class'—Bucky Pizzarelli Guitar Method	Keith Perkins Publishing

SELECTED READING

'7 String Genius'	Robert Yelin, 'Guitar Player', June 1974

COURTESY FESTIVAL RECORDS

Baden Powell

BADEN POWELL

Born—Rio de Janeiro, Brazil

6th August 1937

Baden Powell is regarded by many as the foremost jazz guitarist to come from Brazil since the start of the Bossa Nova boom. He certainly has been one of this idiom's most prolific and successful composers in the last ten years.

Baden's father was a violinist and his grandfather, a Negro fullblood, the conductor of Brazil's first all negro orchestra. His father was also a leader of the Brazilian Boy Scouts, and as a result a great admirer of the founder of the Boy Scout's movement, Robert Thompson Baden Powell. Hence his son was christened Baden Powell after the great scout leader.

On a guitar belonging to his aunt, Baden began playing the guitar at the age of eight. He progressed quickly and was playing professionally at the age of 15. He first gained national prominence in Brazil when he teamed up with the poet Vinicius de Moraes. This popular Brazilian poet has written the lyrics for many of Baden's compositions. Although his guitar playing was founded on the traditional Brazilian music and rhythms Baden loved jazz and he claims his style was greatly influenced by jazz guitarists Django Reinhardt and Barney Kessel.

Although well known inside Brazil, Baden was virtually unknown outside his native country until 1966. German jazz writer Joachim Berendt on a visit to Brazil persuaded Baden to make his first long playing recording following which Baden was to come to Europe.

Since that time Baden's success has grown year after year. He has spent much of his time in Europe although he does go back to Brazil regularly to record and give concerts. He has also played in the U.S.A. with jazz artists such as Stan Getz. Today he is still enormously popular all over Europe and his many recordings are widely available.

SELECTED RECORDS

'Tristeza'	MPS	68—093
'Poema'	MPS	68—089
'Canto'	MPS	68—157
'Estudos'	MPS	68—092
'Images'	MPS	68—091
'Apaixonado'	MPS	68—090
'Le Monde Musical Vol. 1'	Barclay	80—235
'Le Monde Musical Vol. 2'	Barclay	80—385
'Aquarelles de Bresil'	Barclay	80—416
'Baden Powell Quartet Vol. 1'	Barclay	80—428
'Baden Powell Quartet Vol. 2'	Barclay	80—429
'La Cover de Baden Powell'	Festival	FLD 633
'Stephane Grapelli/Baden Powell'	Festival	FLD 634
'Baden Powell'	Fontana	6488—025

SELECTED MUSIC

'Guitar Solos Vol. 1'—Baden Powell	Tonos International Co.

JOE PUMA

Born— JOSEPH J. PUMA
New York City

13th August 1927

Joe Puma with Chuck Wayne (right).

Joe Puma's father and two brothers were guitarists. He originally began working as an aircraft mechanic in 1944 and then as a draughtsman from 1945–7. It was in 1948 whilst living in New York that Joe decided to become a professional musician.

For a period of five years he worked with a variety of small groups including those led by Cy Coleman in 1951 and Sammy Kaye in 1952. After this his guitar talent was featured in a wide assortment of jazz groups including Artie Shaw, Louis Bellson, and Don Eliot. In 1954 he joined singer Peggy Lee

for two years and then led his own group in 1957.

Joe continued playing in mainly small groups, including that of Lee Konitz in 1958, until 1960 when he went on tour as the accompanist to singer Morgana King.

In recent years, despite a bout of ill health, Joe has continued to work in and around New York City, and together with Chuck Wayne he formed an outstanding guitar duo which has recorded and been much in demand in several New York jazz clubs.

SELECTED RECORDS

'Joe Puma Jazz'	Jubilee	JLP 1070
'Wild Kitten'	Dawn	1118
'East Coast Jazz 3'	London	LZ–N14033
'Fourmost Guitars'	ABC Paramount	ABC 109
'Interactions' (duo with Chuck Wayne)	Choice	CRS 1004

SELECTED MUSIC

'Joe Puma Guitar Solos'	Juma Publishing Co.

SELECTED READING

'Magical Jazz Duo'	Ray Gogerty, 'Guitar Player', March 1974

164

SNOOZER QUINN

Born—EDWIN McINTOSH QUINN
McComb, Mississippi, U.S.A. 18th October 1906

Died—New Orleans, Louisiana, 1952

Snoozer Quinn

Snoozer Quinn's early recordings, which showed his true talent on the guitar, are today not available. Fortunately his old friend cornettist Johnny Wiggs recorded Snoozer in 1950 when the guitarist was in hospital and bearing in mind that Quinn was very ill, this record testifies to the fact that Quinn's reputation, as a jazz guitarist of importance, are true.

Snoozer played the mandolin, guitar and violin from the age of seven. His family moved to Bogalusa, Louisiana, and whilst he was in his early teens he was already playing professionally. At the age of 17 he went on the road with the Paul English Travelling Shows. A little later he was featured with Mart Britt's orchestra.

In 1925 he joined his first jazz group 'Peck's Bad Boys' in Shreveport. From late 1925 until 1928 Snoozer played in and around New Orleans. On the recommendation of Bix Beiderbecke and Frankie Trumbauer he was hired by Paul Whiteman. It was during this period with Whiteman that Snoozer developed a terrific reputation amongst his fellow musicians. He played in various night spots often until the early hours of the morning, and it was then that other top jazz artists in New York would get together to hear Quinn's jazz guitar.

In 1929, Snoozer left the Whiteman band and returned home to New Orleans. His health was in very poor shape and although he did some work with local bands his professional days with top line outfits was finished. After suffering many years of ill health Snoozer died in 1952.

SELECTED RECORD
'The Legendary Snoozer Quinn'   Fat Cat Jazz Records   FCJ 104

Jimmy Raney

COURTESY GUITAR/PHOTO GEORGE CLINTON

JIMMY RANEY

Born— JAMES ELBERT RANEY
Louisville, Kentucky, U.S.A.

20th August 1927

Jimmy Raney reached world wide recognition in the nineteen fifties as one of the few really great jazz guitarists. Until recently he had dropped out of the limelight but fortunately for jazz, he has made a comeback in the last few years and is once more playing to jazz audiences throughout the world. There is no doubt that his melodic, inventive and lyrical style has proved to be one of the most influential in jazz guitar history to-date.

Jimmy's father was a well-known sportswriter for a Louisville newspaper. His mother played the guitar and it was she that encouraged an early start for her son on the instrument. She gave him his first lessons and then later whilst at school he studied the classical guitar with A. J. Giancola.

At the age of thirteen he began to study with a local jazz guitarist Hayden Causey who encouraged Jimmy to listen to top jazz guitarists of the time, including Charlie Christian, on records. By the time he was 15 Jimmy was already playing professionally and determined to make the guitar and jazz his career.

In 1944 he joined the Jerry Wald band in New York and was able to hear at first hand the legendary leaders of the modern jazz movement including Art Tatum, Charlie Parker, and Dizzy Gillespie. Between 1945 and 1948 Jimmy played in various combos in Chicago until at the recommendation of drummer 'Tiny' Kahn he was invited to join the Woody Herman band. The band included at that time artists such as Stan Getz and Serge Chaloff with whom Jimmy was to later make several important recordings. In 1949 Jimmy left the Herman band and took up residence with fellow guitarists Tal Farlow and Sal Salvador, and also vibist Teddy Charles. For the next year or so he played with Artie Shaw and the Terry Gibbs' Combo.

Stan Getz, by this time, had become regarded as one of the world's most outstanding tenor saxophone players and after a tour of Sweden he returned to the States to form a new quartet which featured Jimmy on guitar. Stan had a great respect for the Raney style of jazz and together they developed much original and beautiful music.

In 1953 he joined the Red Norvo Trio, touring throughout the United States and Europe in the following year with jazz singer Billie Holiday. In 1954 and 1955 several jazz critics in their annual polls, voted him the 'World's Best Jazz Guitarist'.

Although Jimmy in early years had travelled widely abroad he gradually developed a great dislike for travel, and in particular he abhorred aeroplanes. This was to greatly reduce his 'live' audience particularly as he had decided to stay near to his home with his wife Lee, and his children. In 1955 he joined the Jimmy Lyon trio at the Blue Angel in New York. For the next six years Jimmy remained in New York alternating work between Broadway shows, radio and television work, and club dates. Although he made many fine recordings under his own name and with other artists, including Stan Getz, Bob Brookmeyer and guitarist Jim Hall, Jimmy felt he did not have at that time the staying power to make a successful career for himself as a jazz guitarist. In 1959 he took up the serious study of the cello, and he also studied composition with pianist Hal Overton. He continued his working career for many months accompanying singers such as Tony Bennet, Andy Williams, and Anita O'Day. He was also involved in making several valuable instructional records for the Music Minus One series in New York.

Between 1964 and 1972 little was heard of Jimmy as he had returned to his home town Louisville and was virtually retired from the music scene. Fortunately he now seems to have overcome many of his early problems, including that of travelling. He now spends a good deal of the year touring the world playing in jazz clubs and concerts.

He has also made many new recordings including some with his son Doug who is also a guitarist, and pianist Al Haig.

Jimmy Raney was never a strong chordal soloist on the guitar. But his single note playing makes him one of the most musically creative and brilliant jazz guitarists to-date, having directly inspired many other leading guitarists such as René Thomas, Jimmy Gourley, and Joe Puma.

SELECTED RECORDS

'Red Norvo Trio' Vol. 2	Vogue	LDE 115
'Stan Getz Quintet/Quartet'	Jazz Tone	1230
'Jimmy Raney Quartet'	Esquire	20—070
'Jimmy Raney Plays'	Esquire	20—054
'Guitaristic'	Swing	CLD 882
'Jimmy Raney and George Wallington'	Metronome	ULS 1607E
'Jimmy Raney'	ABC Paramount	ABC 129
'Fourmost Guitars'	ABC Paramount	ABC 109
'Three Attitudes'	HM4	CLP 1264
'Street Swingers' with Jim Hall	Vogue	LAE 12147
'Two Jims and a Zoot'	Fontana	TL 5292
'Strings and Swings'	Muse	5004
'Strings Attached'	Choice	CRS 1010
'Raney/Haig Special Brew'	Spotlite	LP8
'The Influence'	Xanadu	116
'Live in Tokyo'	Xanadu	132
'Jimmy Raney—Solo'	Xanadu	140

SELECTED MUSIC

'For Guitarists Only' (with record)	Music Minus One 4009

SELECTED READING

'Jimmy Raney'	Ira Gitler, 'Downbeat', 20th July 1961
'Jimmy Raney'	Arnie Berle, 'Guitar Player', March 1977
'The Incomparable Jimmy Raney'	George Clinton, 'Guitar', July 1977

Jimmy Raney

COURTESY XANADU RECORDS/PHOTO DON SCHLITTEN

ERNEST RANGLIN

Born—Manchester, Jamaica

1933

Ernest Ranglin

Today, Ernest Ranglin is hardly known outside Jamaica, but on his few visits to Europe and the U.K. he has astounded jazz lovers by his amazing ability on the guitar. He briefly appeared at Ronnie Scott's jazz club in London in the late nineteen sixties and his jazz records made at that time on the 'Island' label bear testimony to his fine jazz guitar work.

Today he is once more based on his native islands playing in clubs and hotels. He has been associated recently with jazz pianist Monty Alexander and in fact recorded with him on a trip to Germany in 1974. This record, which has just been released on the MPS label, once more shows that the guitar virtuosity of Ernest Ranglin should not be ignored.

SELECTED RECORDS

'Wranglin'	Island	ILP 909
'Reflections'	Island	ILP 915
'Ranglypso'	MPS	15—440

Django Reinhardt

DJANGO REINHARDT

Born— JEAN BAPTISTE REINHARDT Liverchies, Belgium,
23rd January 1910

Died—Fontainebleu, France, 16th May 1953

A legend in his own time and even a greater legend today. There are few guitarists (either jazz or classical) throughout the world who have not heard of Django and no doubt most guitarists will have at least one of his recordings in their collection.

Django was born into a gypsy family, and as a child roamed through Belgium and France as a member of a caravan, gaining a great knowledge of the guitar, banjo and violin. On 2nd November 1928 he was caught in a terrible fire in his caravan which had been camped on the outskirts of Paris. Although he and his first wife succeeded in escaping the fire Django suffered severe burns of his hands and body. After hospital treatment he was left with two withered fingers on his left hand. To most guitarists this would have spelt doom to any further thoughts of a musical career. But not Django, who with the combination of great determination and physical strength succeeded in developing a unique technique which established him as the most outstanding jazz guitarist of his time.

Although Django could use his withered fourth and fifth fingers for some very simple chords on the first two strings he could never use them for his outstanding single string runs. The brilliant solos that he played, often at the most astonishing speed, were played entirely with the first two fingers of his left hand.

His early jazz playing has been described as 'Provencale, flaming in colourful decoration' yet in his later years his music was most definitely influenced by the great post war top musicians that Django heard on recordings and during his concert tour of America. A most fascinating personality, Django was a true gypsy. He could be a most charming yet awkward character. Although often unreliable in his attendances at concerts and recording sessions he was able to reach momentous heights of greatness in his musical inventions and artistry.

Django was a natural musician, and even if he could have read music he would still probably have preferred to improvise. As well as jazz, he had great love for all good music. He loved colour which was not only reflected in his often garish and flamboyant dress but also in his hobby of oil painting, as well as his music.

After playing with various musicians, Django joined Stephane Grapelli in 1934 and they formed their historic 'Quintette Du Hot Club De France', a group which consisted of three guitars, one violin, and one double bass. The unique sound they produced is still today emulated by various well-known groups throughout the world. Django used almost exclusively throughout his career several of the French-made Maccaferri guitars, easily recognizable by their distinctive shape and sound, although in his latter years he sometimes used various American-made electric guitars which had been presented to him by the makers. From 1935 as the popularity of the 'Hot Club' grew to world-wide proportions, they made recording after recording and toured throughout Europe and Britain. Almost every great American jazzman of the time made a point when visiting Paris, to seek out and play with the legendary Django. He was one of the few great and original jazz musicians that Europe has ever produced. Amongst these visiting musicians were Coleman Hawkins, Benny Carter, Bill Coleman, Dickie Wells and Rex Stewart. The 'Hot Club' has been regarded by many jazz observers as probably the most important influence in the pioneering of jazz in Europe and Britain up to 1945.

After the war Django, constantly aware of the new movements in jazz and music generally, played with various new combinations of small and big groups which have been equally well recorded as the earlier 'Hot Club' Quintet. One of his many compositions 'Nuages' reached the hit parade in several countries and today is still a favourite solo piece for the jazz guitarist.

Unfortunately, as with many other great men of genius, death came all too early to Django. In May 1953 he suffered a stroke after an afternoon of fishing on the bank of the river Seine and within a few hours Django was dead. The world had lost one of its most outstanding jazz guitarists and musicians.

Django Circa 1930

COURTESY MARIO MACCAFERRI

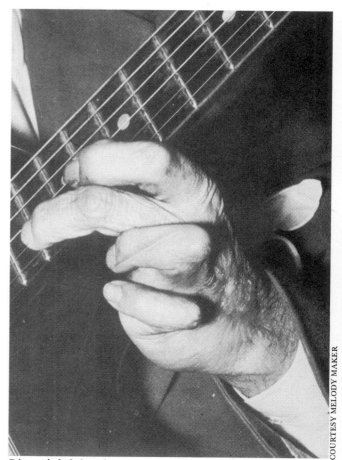

Django's left hand

COURTESY MELODY MAKER

Django May 1953

172

Django's grave at Samois.

COURTESY MELODY MAKER

Today Django's following is greater than ever, his records still outsell those of nearly all other jazz guitarists. Books have been written about him, transcriptions of his solos are available, and magazines regularly feature articles on him. All over the world groups and guitarists still try to reproduce his unique sounds, and it is generally agreed that no other guitarist of any style, appeals to such a wide variety of guitarists as Django.

SELECTED RECORDS

Django recorded for several companies and over the last few years they have re-issued most of his recordings in special sets, as well as in single volumes. All of Django's recordings are of importance and these are listed in full in Max Abrams' 'Book of Django'. For convenience I list below what I feel are the most important selections of Django's recordings.

'Reinhardt Selection'	Pathe/EMI	20 Records	Pathe/Marconi	054—160001/160020
'Reinhardt Selection'	Vogue	5 Records	Vogue	COF 03
'Reinhardt Selection'	RCA	3 Records	Black and White	FXM3 7055
'Reinhardt Selection'	Decca	5 Records	Decca	115—120/124
'Reinhardt Selection'	Capitol	2 Records	Capitol	10226
'Reinhardt Selection'	Barclay	2 Records	Barclay	80—929/30
'Django'			Polydor	236510
'Bruxelles 48'			Vogue	LDM 30217
'Django—The Later Years'			La Roulotte	MA—3

SELECTED MUSIC

'A Treasury of Django Reinhardt'	76 Solos	Jewel Publishing Co.
'L 'Inoubliable Django'	15 Solos	Francis Day SA
'Magic of Django' Vol. 1	10 Solos	Francis Day and Hunter
'Magic of Django' Vol. 2	10 Solos	Francis Day and Hunter
'Django—Souvenir' Vol. 1	10 Solos	Francis Day SA
'Django—Souvenir' Vol. 2	10 Solos	Francis Day SA
'Django's 30 Finest Solos—Note for Note'	Paul Visvader	

SELECTED READING

'Django Reinhardt'	Chas Delaunay—Cassell 1961 (Biography in English)
'Django—Mon Frere'	Chas Delaunay—'La Terrain Vogue' (Biography in French)
'The Book of Django'	Max Abrams 1973
'The Rebirth of Django's Guitar'	M. J. Summerfield—CSL Co. 1975
'Guitar Player'	November 1976 is a special Django issue
'The Fabulous Gypsy'	'Esquire Book of Jazz'—Arthur Barker Ltd. 1963
'Djangologie'	Clive N. Cooper, 'Jazz Journal', June 1971
'Barney Kessel Remembers Reinhardt'	'Downbeat', 25th June 1959
'The Magnificent Django'	George Hoefer, 'Downbeat', 14th July 1966
'Remembering Django'	Dennis E. Hersley, 'Downbeat', 26th February 1976
'Django Reinhardt—Ein Portrait'	Dr. Dieter Schultz-Kohn—'Jazz Bucherei No. 6'
'Django—Une Legende Toujours Vivante'	'Jazz Magazine' (France) May 1970
'Gypsy—Dinosaurs in the Morning'	Whitney Balliett p. 86—91
'Django Reinhardt'	'Jazz' p. 29—39, Graham Collier, Cambridge University Press
'Django Reinhardt'	Bob Rovai, 'Guitar Player', June 1969
'Django—A Dedication'	Carey Blyton, 'B.M.G.' March 1973
'The Maccaferri-Django's Guitar'	Paul Shekasky, 'Guitar Player', April 1974
'Django'	Stephane Grappeli, 'Guitar', November 1973

Left to right, Django, Jack Teagarden, Stephane Grapelli and Earl Hines.

COURTESY MELODY MAKER

173

Django Reinhardt

COURTESY MELODY MAKER

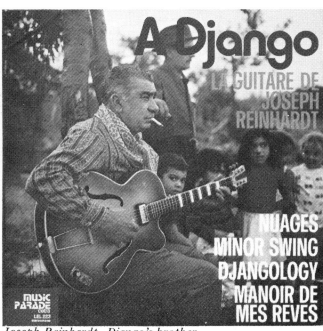

Joseph Reinhardt—Django's brother.

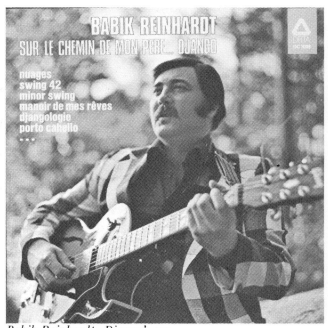

Babik Reinhardt—Django's son.

174

ALLAN REUSS

Born—New York City, U.S.A.

15th June 1915

Allan Reuss with Bunny Berigan's Band 1939.

COURTESY JAZZ JOURNAL

Allan Reuss is looked upon by many musicians as one of the best rhythm guitarists America has produced. His swinging guitar style has been the mainstay of some of the finest big bands from the nineteen thirties through to the nineteen fifties.

Reuss originally started on the banjo at the age of 12. He changed to the guitar and studied for a while under George Van Eps, who eventually recommended that Alan should take his place in the Benny Goodman orchestra.

From 1934—8 Allan toured with the Goodman band. After this he played with Jack Teagarden until 1940, Jimmy Dorsey 1941—2, and the N.B.C. band in Chicago from 1942—3. He went back to the Goodman band for a while in 1943 and then joined the Harry James band until 1944.

He was rarely featured as a soloist but Allan was capable of playing punchy chordal and single string solos, much in the style of Dick McDonough. His superb recorded solo 'Picking for Patsy' with the Jack Teagarden orchestra in 1939 bears witness to this. In recent years Allan has freelanced around Los Angeles and also spends a lot of time teaching.

SELECTED RECORDS

'Benny Goodman and his Orchestra'	Jazz Anthology	30JA 5151
'Goodman at the Cotton Club 1938'	Jazz Archives	JA 12
'This is Benny Goodman'	RCA	VPM 6063
'Jack Teagarden and his Big Band 1939'	TAX	M—8024
'Coleman Hawkins—Hollywood Stampede'	Pathe Marconi	CO 62 80802

SELECTED MUSIC

'Allan Reuss's Guitar Solos'	ABC Music Corporation

SELECTED READING

'Allan Reuss'	Ivor Mairants, 'Guitar', May 1974

LEE RITENOUR

Born— LEE MACK RITENOUR
Hollywood, California, U.S.A.

1st November 1952

Lee Ritenour

COURTESY STRINGS 'N' THINGS

Lee Ritenour is today regarded by many musicians as one of the most musically talented guitarists based in Los Angeles.

Lee began to play the guitar at the age of eight and diligently studied his chosen instrument. By the time he was only 12 he was already featured in a 19 piece band called 'The Esquires' and at 17 he quickened his progress on the guitar by studying with jazz guitarists Joe Pass and Howard Roberts, as well as classical player Christopher Parkening.

His first major professional break came when he joined the Sergio Mendes band, 'Brazil 66'. His travels with this outfit took him as far as Japan. On

his return to Los Angeles he was often featured with guitarist John Pisano at the 'Donte's' club, which had a regular guitar night.

Today Lee is very busy in the Los Angeles studios and his youthful, vigorous, jazz/rock style is much in demand for recordings. After the death of Jack Marshall, Lee took on the tutorship of Marshall's guitar workshop at the University of Southern California. Amongst the names of the many top musicians with whom Lee has recently recorded are Herbie Hancock, Peggy Lee, Gato Barbieri, and Oliver Nelson.

SELECTED RECORDS

'First Course'	Epic	PE 33947
'Captain Fingers'	Epic	PE 34426
'Guitar Player'	MCA	2—6002

SELECTED READING

'Lee Ritenour'	Frankie Nemko, 'Guitar Player', August 1975
'Lee Ritenour'	Joan Levine, 'Downbeat', 13th March 1975

TONY RIZZI

Born– TREFONI RIZZI
Los Angeles, California, U.S.A.

16th April 1923

Tony Rizzi (centre) with the Five Guitars.

The guitar was Tony Rizzi's third choice of musical instruments. He studied the violin for 11 years, then changed to the trumpet and finally to the guitar. After leaving the Army, Tony played with many name bands including those of Les Brown and Boyd Raeburn.

In recent years he has been mainly involved as a staff musician for the N.B.C., and also television and film work. He has always been deeply interested in jazz and the music of Charlie Christian and this resulted in the formation in 1973 of a group headed by five guitars. This group has recently recorded a record devoted entirely to harmonized versions for five guitars of Christian's solos, taken note for note from Benny Goodman records.

SELECTED RECORDS

'Tony Rizzi's Five Guitars Play Charlie Christian	Milagro	1000
'Disco Pacific'–The Five Guitars	Outstanding Records	—
'Surfin' Pacific'–The Five Guitars	Outstanding Records	—

SELECTED READING

'Tony Rizzi's Five Guitars'	Frankie R. Nemko, 'Guitar Player', December 1976

COURTESY JAZZ JOURNAL

Howard Roberts

HOWARD ROBERTS

Born – HOWARD MANCEL ROBERTS
Phoenix, Arizona, U.S.A.

2nd October 1929

Howard Roberts began playing the guitar at an early age. By the time he was 12 he was under the tutelage of Horace Hutchett who inspired the young guitarist with a love for the full spectrum of the guitar, from jazz to classical.

During the second World War Howard gigged in and around Phoenix and so gained valuable professional experience. In 1950 following in the footsteps of many other musicians Howard decided to move to Los Angeles where he soon established himself as a leading studio musician. He has since then remained there becoming one of the most respected guitarists in America. He has been featured on literally thousands of recordings and in many television and film soundtracks.

Howard has written, in collaboration with fellow guitarist Jimmy Stewart, some excellent and important jazz guitar books. He holds several guitar seminars throughout the U.S.A. every year and this also has proved a great contribution from Howard to America's young guitarists. He was also very active in establishing the guitar night at Donte's club in 1966. He now also writes an excellent monthly column in 'Guitar Player' magazine. His latest recording work has been influenced by the jazz/rock movement of the seventies but his recordings from the nineteen sixties show his all-round jazz ability on the guitar.

SELECTED RECORDS

'Movin' Man'	ESP	29
'Mr. Roberts Plays Guitar'	Verve	MGV 8192
'Velvet Groove'	Verve	8662
'Julie is her Name' Vol. 2	London	HA–V 2186
'Good Picking'	Verve	MGV 8305
'Colour him Funky'	Capitol	ST1887
'Guilty'	Capitol	2824
'Equinox Express Elevator'	ABC/Impulse	Impl 8004
'The Real Howard Roberts'	Concord	CJ 53

SELECTED MUSIC

'Howard Roberts Chord Melody'	Playback Publishing Co.
'Howard Roberts Guitar Book'	Playback Publishing Co.
'Howard Roberts Sight Reading for the Guitar'	Playback Publishing Co.

SELECTED READING

'Mr. Roberts'	'Guitar Player', August 1967
'Howard Roberts' Binary Bag'	Harvey Siders, 'Downbeat', 29th June 1967
'Profile of a Pro'	'Guitar Player', April 1970

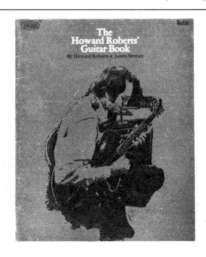

TERJE RYPDAL

Born—Oslo, Norway

23rd August 1947

Terje Rypdal

Both Rypdal's parents are musical. His father Jakop is a captain in a military band, and his mother Inger-Lise a pop singer. Terje started his musical training on the piano at the age of five and began to play the guitar when he reached 13. His first professional work was with a rock group, his major influence at that time being Hank Marvin and the 'Shadows'.

In 1968 Terje gained his first real jazz experience playing with a group led by Jan Garbarek. This break made the young Norwegian guitarist decide to make music his career. In 1969 he furthered his musical studies under the guidance of the Norwegian composer, Finn Mortenson. For some time classical composers such as Mahler were his main influence but at the same time Terje listened to many jazz records and was influenced by a variety of top jazz guitarists including Charlie Christian. Wes Montgomery and Kenny Burrell.

It was in 1969 that Terje gained his first international recognition when he appeared in a free jazz festival at Baden Baden in West Germany. Although in 1972 Rypdal began to play both the flute and soprano-saxophone, the guitar still remained his main instrument. He led his own group called 'Odyssey' in 1975 and this received a warm reception at concerts both in Europe and the United Kingdom, and so furthered his popularity as one of the world's foremost jazz/rock guitarists and composers.

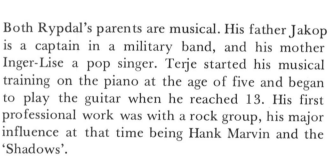

SELECTED RECORDS

'Terje Rypdal'	ECM	1016ST
'What comes After'	ECM	1031ST
'Odyssey'	ECM	1067/68
'After the Rain'	ECM	1—1083
'Dream'	Karusell Gold	2915 068

SELECTED READING

'Terje Rypdal' Jon Sievert, 'Guitar Player', May 1977

JOHNNY ST CYR

Born— JOHN ALEXANDER ST CYR
New Orleans, Louisiana, U.S.A. 17th April 1890

Died—Los Angeles, California, U.S.A.
17th June 1966

Johnny St. Cyr

Johnny St. Cyr played both banjo and guitar throughout his long career in jazz. Basically a rhythm player he was associated with many of the great names of traditional jazz including Louis Armstrong, Kid Ory and Jelly Roll Morton.

His father played both the guitar and flute and Johnny was playing professionally by the time he was 15, although his main profession during the daytime was as a plasterer He played in several well-known groups in New Orleans including those of Papa Celestin and Kid Ory, and for many years he played off and on with Armand Piron. He also did riverboat work with Fate Marable and Ed Allen.

Johnny moved to Chicago in 1923 playing with King Oliver and then for five years with Doc Cook's Dreamland orchestra. During his time with Cook he was much in demand for freelance recording sessions, with Louis Armstrong, Jelly Roll Morton, and other top jazzmen of the time.

He returned to New Orleans in late 1929 and then for many years he left the music scene to take up plastering again, although he did do part time playing at night. It was not until the nineteen fifties that he decided to go back into music full time.

He joined Paul Barbarin's band and in 1955 moved to California with him. In 1959 he was featured with the New Orleans Creole Jazz Band and then the Young Men of New Orleans in the early nineteen sixties. He was involved in a car accident in 1965 and this affected his ability to play on a regular basis. He died in 1966 of leukaemia in Los Angeles.

SELECTED RECORD
'Jelly Roll Morton'   RCA Black and White   731 059

SELECTED READING
'Jazz as I Remember' Part 1   Johnny St Cyr—'Jazz Journal', September 1966
'Jazz as I Remember' Part 2   Johnny St Cyr—'Jazz Journal', October 1966

Sal Salvador

SAL SALVADOR

Born—Monson, Massachussetts, U.S.A.

21st November 1925

The Salvador family moved to Stafford Springs in Connecticut in 1927. Sal's first guitar was given to him by his father, and his first musical interest, like many of his friends, was hillbilly music.

During the nineteen forties Sal heard, and was influenced by, the jazz guitar of Charlie Christian. Although he already had an appreciation of jazz because of his love of Harry James' trumpet style. He first studied the acoustic styles of Dick McDonough, Carl Kress, and George Van Eps but on hearing Charlie Christian Sal decided to develop his style on the electric guitar. He benefited by taking correspondence courses with Oscar Moore and Hy Whyte, and also personal lessons from guitarist Eddie Smith.

In 1949 his friend and fellow guitarist Mundell Lowe recommended him for the position of staff guitarist at the Radio City Music Hall in New York. He also developed a friendship with Johnny Smith who was then the N.B.C. staff guitarist, and so Sal further enlarged his knowledge of the guitar.

After leaving Radio City Sal went on the road, first with vibist Terry Gibbs, and then with Eddie Best and a group called 'The Dardanelles'. On his return to New York Sal formed a jazz quartet with Mundell Lowe.

The next few years found Salvador mainly involved with the Columbia Recording Company, backing artists such as Marlene Dietrich, Frankie Lane, Tony Bennett, and Rosemary Clooney. In 1952 Sal joined the legendary Stan Kenton orchestra and for two years he played a prominent part in the sound of the early Kenton band.

In 1954 Sal formed his own group with pianist Eddie Costa. This quartet recorded and gained popularity touring top jazz clubs throughout the U.S.A. He was a featured soloist at the Newport Jazz Festival in 1958 and for a while fronted his own big band 'The Colours of Sound'. This latter venture unfortunately coincided with the decline of the big band scene and as a result suffered the same end as virtually all the other big bands at the time.

Sal is currently involved on the East coast of the U.S.A. with publishing, and his jazz playing is mainly heard in a duo with guitarist Allen Hanlon.

SELECTED RECORDS

'Shades of Sal Salvador'	Bethlehem	39
'Sal Salvador Quintet'	Blue Note	BLP 5035
'Sal Salvador'	Capitol	KPL 105
'Frivolous Sal'	London	HA—N 2043
'Colours in Sound'	Decca	DL 79210
'Beat for this Generation'	Decca	DL 74026
'Live' Duo with Alan Hanlon'	Glen Productions	GPSA 5010

SELECTED MUSIC

'Sal Salvador's Chord Book'	Henry Adler Music Publishers
'Sal Salvador's Single String Studies'	Henry Adler Music Publishers
'Jazz Guitar Duets'	Belwin Music Inc.

SELECTED READING

'A Jazz Great for Thirty Years'	Richard Albero, 'Guitar Player', July 1974

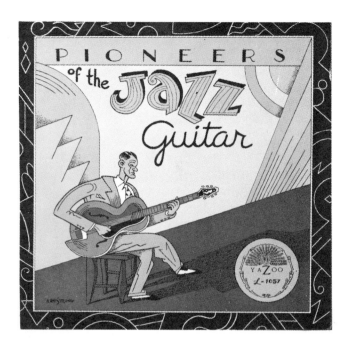

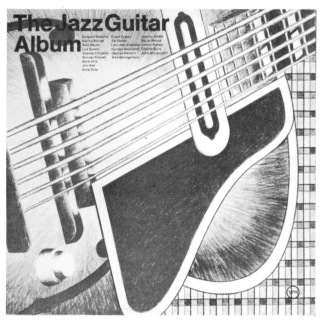

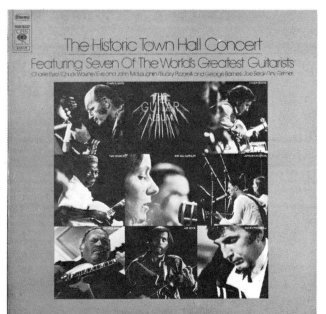

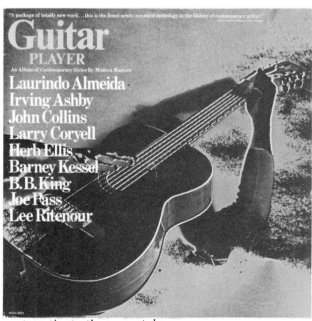

A selection of fine jazz guitar solos and duos on record from the nineteen-twenties to the present day.

BUD SCOTT

Born– ARTHUR SCOTT New Orleans, Louisiana, U.S.A.
11th January 1890

Died–Los Angeles, California, U.S.A. 2nd July 1949

Bud Scott with the Kid Ory Band.

Bud Scott was mainly featured as a member of the rhythm section on both guitar and banjo, of many jazz groups from the beginning of the twentieth century. He is an important figure in the evolution of the jazz guitar as he was a direct link from the early blues singer/guitarists of the late nineteenth century right through to the middle of the twentieth century.

Scott learned to play both the guitar and violin from an early age. At the age of 14 he was already playing with the John Robichaux orchestra in New Orleans. In 1913 he took the job as featured violinist with the Billy King travelling show and in 1915 he moved to New York. Here he led a wide and varied career. He not only played banjo with the Bob Young band but sang at a Carnegie Hall concert with the Clef Club in 1919. Scott was also much in demand for theatre work whilst he was in New York.

In 1923 Bud moved to Chicago where he joined the legendary King Oliver. For a while he lived in California and started what would be a long association with trombonist Kid Ory. Scott returned to Chicago in 1926 and rejoined King Oliver and over the next few years worked with many top jazz artists including Erskine Tate and Jimmie Noone.

Bud decided in 1929 to make his home in Los Angeles and during the thirties worked with bands led by Mutt Carey and Leon Herriford. As well as doing a lot of freelance work, including film studio jobs, Bud led his own trio for several years. In 1944 he rejoined Kid Ory with whose band he was mainly associated until he died in 1949.

SELECTED RECORD
'Jelly Roll Morton'   RCA Black and White   731 059

BOLA SETE

Born— DJALMA DE ANDRADA
Rio de Janeiro, Brazil

16th July 1928

Bola Sete

Coming from a musical family, Bola studied theory and harmony at the National School of Music in Rio de Janeiro. His first professional work on the guitar was playing in a folk group. He became interested in jazz and decided to return to the conservatory to further his musical studies in general.

Sete then became a staff guitarist for three radio stations in Rio until he decided to move to the U.S.A. in 1960. For two years he remained unrecognized by the American jazz public and he made his living by playing at various Sheraton Hotels. He was fortunate to be heard by trumpeter Dizzy Gillespie, who asked him to play at the Monterey Jazz Festival in 1962. He then recorded with Dizzy and as a result won a contract with Fantasy records.

For three years from 1963 Sete was featured in the trio of jazz pianist Vince Guaraldi. He was also seen and heard in many radio and television shows, as well as doing some film work. The year 1966 saw the formation of his own group which played successfully all over the U.S.A. for three years, and in 1971 he also led a quartet.

Today Bola Sete is mainly heard as a soloist both on the guitar, and lutar (a lute shaped guitar of his own design), and is generally recognized as one of the most important and individual jazz guitarists to come from the South American continent.

SELECTED RECORDS

'New Wave' with Dizzy Gillespie	Mercury	MGW 12318
'Bola Sete—Bossa Nova'	Fantasy	3349
'The Incomparable Bola Sete'	Fantasy	8364
'Bola Sete's Tour De Force'	Fantasy	8358
'Live at Monterey'	Verve	SVLP 9208
'Ocean'—Solos by Bola Sete	Sonet	SNTF 695

SELECTED READING

'Bola Sete'	Dave McCarthy, 'Guitar Player', December 1967
'Latin Love Affair—Bola Sete'	Russ Wilson, 'Downbeat', 14th July 1966
'Bola Sete'	John Fahey, 'Guitar Player', February 1976

JIMMY SHIRLEY

Born JAMES ARTHUR SHIRLEY
Union, South Carolina, U.S.A.

31st May 1913

Jimmy Shirley

Due mainly to the energetic jazz orientated French recording company 'Black and Blue', the name Jimmy Shirley is once more becoming familiar to jazz lovers throughout the world. Although in the nineteen thirties and early forties he was regarded as one of the most active guitarists on the jazz scene.

Jimmy spent most of his childhood in Cleveland, Ohio, and received his first musical education from his father. In 1935 he was already leading his own quartet made up of three guitars and a double bass. The previous year he had already gained valuable experience with the bands of Frank Terry and Hal Draper in Cincinnati.

In 1937 Jimmy moved to New York and joined the Clarence Profit Trio for four years. Following this successful venture the guitarist toured with singer Ella Fitzgerald for two years. For a period of almost 10 years from 1944 Jimmy was mainly associated with pianist Herman Chittison in various clubs in New York City. Right through to the sixties Jimmy was constantly featured and heard with well known jazz names including Phil Moore, Billy Williams, Vin Strong and 'Toy' Wilson.

Until recently Jimmy Shirley was still working regularly in and around New York on both guitar and electric bass guitar, with artists such as saxophonists Buddy Tate and George James. His recent recordings on 'Black and Blue' will hopefully ensure that the guitar work of Jimmy Shirley is not ignored.

SELECTED RECORDS

'China Boy'—Jimmy Shirley	Black and Blue	33 081
'Steff and Slam'	Black and Blue	33 076

ROY SMECK

Born—Binghampton, New York, U.S.A.

1900

Roy Smeck

COURTESY ROY SMECK

Roy Smeck originally played a variety of instruments including the autoharp and harmonica. His father sang and played the guitar and it was on his father's instrument that Roy started to play the guitar. Although not really a jazz artist Smeck is included in this book as there is no doubt of his influence on many jazz guitarists, via his recordings and tutors. He is also the only major plectrum guitarist from the nineteen twenties still living today.

By the mid-twenties Smeck was already recording for R.C.A. After being heard in the music store where he was working by a R.K.O. theatre agent he was persuaded to go to New York City for an audition. He was immediately signed up and he commenced a long and highly successful music hall career as 'The Wizard of the Strings'. In 1928 he was hired by Warner Brothers to make one of the first talking movies a seven minute film called 'Roy Smeck in his Pastime'. Roy was not only a top line guitarist but he also was a master of the banjo, ukulele and Hawaiian guitar.

Smeck in fact was the first artist to make use of multiple recording. He made a film for Paramount playing four different instruments and by the use of overdubbing the audience saw and heard all four instruments playing at once when the film was shown.

For many years in fact right through to the nineteen fifties, Roy Smeck was a big name in variety shows throughout the world. He appeared at the London Palladium in 1937, and in 1938 he was one of the first artists featured on English television. Roy had already become a radio star in the U.S.A. having been booked to give a daily fifteen minute guitar lesson on the radio in New York in 1936.

Since the nineteen fifties Roy has settled in New York and has been mainly involved in the teaching of all fretted instruments, although he still does occasional cabaret, radio and television work. During his long career Roy Smeck has made over 500 recordings and has also written 30 books on various fretted instruments. There is no doubt that his contribution to the guitar in general has been enormous.

SELECTED RECORD
'Roy Smeck Plays'   Yazoo   YZ1052

SELECTED MUSIC
'Blues for Guitar'   Roy Smeck. Charles Colin Publishing
'Melodious Rhythms Simplified'   Roy Smeck. Charles Colin Publishing

SELECTED READING
'Roy Smeck The Wizard Reminisces'   Robert Yelin, 'Guitar Player', December 1972
'Roy Smeck The Wizard of the Strings'   'B.M.G.' September 1974

FLOYD SMITH

Born—St. Louis, Missouri, U.S.A.

25th January 1917

Floyd Smith

Floyd Smith was the son of a drummer. He studied music at his local high school, his first instrument being the ukulele and then the guitar. His first professional work was on the banjo when he joined Eddie Johnson's Crackerjacks and then Dewey Jackson's band. In 1937 he was featured with the Jeter Pillars orchestra and in 1938 with the Sunset Royal Orchestra.

National prominence came for Floyd when he joined Andy Kirk in January 1939. He made his recording 'Floyds Guitar Blues' on the electric guitar with this band in the same year and this track helped give acceptance to the amplified

instrument. In 1942 he was drafted into the U.S. Army but he returned to work with Kirk after the war in 1945 until September 1946.

For some time he played with his own trio in Chicago and in the mid-nineteen fifties worked in other cities with a variety of jazz artists including organist Wild Bill Davis and drummer Chris Columbus. Recent years have found Floyd, working both in the U.S.A. and Europe and in 1972 he made a record for the French label Black and Blue with his own trio made up of Davis, Columbus, and himself. An up-to-date version of Floyd's Guitar Blues is included on the record.

SELECTED RECORDS

'Andy Kirk Band—Instrumentally Speaking'	MCA	510 033
'Floyd Smith Trio'	Black and Blue	33—046
'Impulsions'—Wild Bill Davis Trio	Black and Blue	33—037

Johnny Smith

COURTESY GUITAR

JOHNNY SMITH

JOHN HENRY SMITH JNR
Born—Birmingham, Alabama, U.S.A.

25th June 1922

Johnny Smith is regarded by many as one of the foremost modern guitarists, yet he is not only a virtuoso guitar player but also extremely accomplished on the trumpet, violin and viola.

A self taught player, who cites Andres Segovia and Django Reinhardt as his major influences, Johnny developed an interest in the guitar from his father who was a banjo player. He originally gained his first professional experience in a hillbilly group called 'The Fenton Brothers' in 1939. He led his own trio in Boston in 1940—1 before joining the forces. During the war he played trumpet in the Air Force Band. On leaving the Air Force he joined the N.B.C. staff in New York in 1947. For six years he played both the trumpet and guitar in all types of groups and orchestras for the network.

He first came to prominence in the jazz world in the nineteen fifties when he formed his own quintet featuring tenor saxophonist Stan Getz. Their arrangement and recording of 'Moonlight in Vermont' has become a jazz classic, epitomising the term 'Cool' jazz, and was one of the best selling jazz records in 1952. Today this record remains a milestone in jazz guitar history, distinguished by the unique harmonies of Johnny Smith's block chording on the guitar.

From 1953—60 Johnny successfully led his own group in East coast jazz clubs. Since then this brilliant guitarist has gone into virtual retirement from the professional music scene devoting much of his time to his own music shop in Colorado Springs, although he recently went on tour with Bing Crosby, just prior to the singer's death in 1977.

SELECTED RECORDS

'Johnny Smith plays Jimmy Van Heusen'	Roost	2201
'Johnny Smith Quartet'	Roost	2203
'Moonlight in Vermont'	Roost	2211
'Moods'	Roost	2215
'The Sound of the Johnny Smith Guitar'	Roost	2216
'Flowerdrum Song'	Roost	2231
'Easy Listening'	Roost	2233
'Johnny Smith Trio Designed for You'	Roost	2238
'My Dear Little Sweetheart'	Roost	2239
'Johnny Smith with Strings'	Roost	2242
'Johnny Smith plus the Trio'	Roost	2243
'Sounds of Johnny Smith'	Roost	2246
'Man with Blue Guitar'	Roost	2248
'Reminiscing'	Roost	2259
'Johnny Smith'	Verve	SVLP 9185
'Kaleidoscope'	Verve	SVLP 9205
'With Jerry Southern'	Roulette	52016

SELECTED MUSIC

'Johnny Smith Aids to Technique'	Chas Colin Publishing Co.
'Johnny Smith Guitar Originals Vol. 1'	Chas Colin Publishing Co.
'Johnny Smith Guitar Originals Vol. 2'	Chas Colin Publishing Co.
'Johnny Smith Approach to the Guitar Vol. 1'	Mel Bay Publications
'Johnny Smith Approach to the Guitar Vol. 2'	Mel Bay Publications

SELECTED READING

'Johnny Smith'	'Guitar Player', October 1967
'Johnny Smith'	Interview—'Guitar Player', March 1970
'King of Good Taste 1'	George Clinton, 'Guitar', August 1976
'King of Good Taste 2'	George Clinton, 'Guitar', September 1976

LES SPANN

Born—LESLIE L. SPANN JUNIOR
Pine Bluff, Arkansas

23rd May 1932

Les Spann

COURTESY GUILD GUITARS

Les Spann came to prominence in the early nineteen sixties both as a jazz guitarist and flautist but in the last few years has not been in the forefront as a jazz guitarist. Les taught himself to play the guitar whilst he was at high school in Jamaica, New York. Deciding that music was to be his career he went to Tennessee State University in Nashville, where he was to major in music in 1956. He chose the flute as his second instrument for the course. Whilst he was in Nashville he played with a local band called the 'Tennessee State Collegians'. In August 1957, he returned to New York to join pianist Phineas Newborn's quartet. A short spell followed with Ronell Bright and in August 1958 he gained his first real jazz exposure when he joined the Dizzy Gillespie quintet for a year. Spann left Gillespie and joined Quincy Jones for a world tour in 1959.

SELECTED RECORD
'Gemini—Les Spann'   Jazzland   JLP 35

SELECTED READING
'After Rock—What?' Les Spann   'Downbeat', 14th July 1966

JIMMY STEWART

Born—JAMES OTTO STEWART
San Francisco, California, U.S.A.

8th September 1937

Jimmy Stewart

COURTESY JIMMY STEWART

Jimmy Stewart is well known to jazz guitarists throughout the world by his excellent monthly column in 'Guitar Player' magazine, and also for his co-operation on projects such as the Howard Roberts guitar books and the Wes Montgomery guitar method. He is also a fine guitarist in his own right spending much of his time in the Los Angeles studios.

Jimmy began to play the guitar at the age of seven, his first attraction to music being some recordings by Django Reinhardt. His music studies were divided between the classics and jazz and by the time he was 16 he was already playing professionally backing vocalists in the San Francisco area.

At the age of 19 he played in Las Vegas and then after leaving the Army Jimmy studied the classical guitar with Richard Pick at the Chicago School of Music.

On his return to San Francisco Stewart was not only accomplished on most fretted instruments, but he had also gained a fine knowledge of the theoretical aspects of music. For three years he worked with the Hungarian guitarist Gabor Szabo, mainly backing him on the nylon string guitar. After a successful performance at one of Donte's Guitar nights Stewart formed his own quartet. He has recently made his first jazz record as leader on the Catalyst label.

SELECTED RECORDS

'The Sorcerer' (with Gabor Szabo)	Impulse	M1PL 506
'Fire Flower'	Catalyst	CAT 7621
'Faces' (with Gabor Szabo)	Mercury	SRM 1—1141

SELECTED READING

'Jimmy Stewart'	Bill Lee, 'Guitar Player', December 1970
'The Complete Musician'	Monthly Article by Jimmy Stewart, 'Guitar Player'

COURTESY GUITAR

Louis Stewart

LOUIS STEWART

Born—Waterford, Eire

5th January 1944

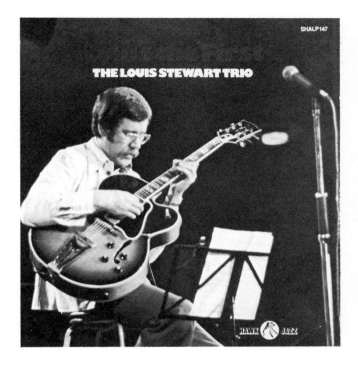

Louis Stewart's early musical experience was on the piano but when he was 15 on hearing a Les Paul record, he decided to buy a guitar. Some time later he heard on a radio jazz programme a record by Barney Kessel and this convinced Louis that jazz was the music for him.

Stewart soon developed a reputation around Dublin as a fine guitarist working with various types of groups. In 1961 he was a member of a band that visited America. After three years doing showband work Louis joined a jazz trio led by pianist Noel Kelehan. This trio played on a very regular basis in and around Dublin and the guitarist's association with Kelehan proved very beneficial, for in the mid-sixties many visiting American jazz musicians to Ireland, including saxophonists Gerry Mulligan and Lee Konitz played with this trio. In 1968 Louis was featured with the Jim Doherty Quartet at the Montreux Jazz Festival and he received the Press Award as the Outstanding European Soloist of this Festival. Shortly after the 1968 Montreux Festival Louis

decided to move to London where he joined a quartet led by the outstanding saxophonist, Tubby Hayes. This gave the Irish guitarist the exposure to top line jazz that he could not get in Ireland. Whilst he was with Hayes, Louis was heard by Benny Goodman who invited him to join his big band for three European tours. This gave Stewart many more valuable new jazz contacts, particularly with American jazz musicians.

In 1971 Louis returned to Dublin and spent much of his time in television and recording work. The music he wrote for television included that for the award winning programme 'A Week in the Life of Martin Cluxton'.

In mid-1975 Stewart joined Ronnie Scott's new quartet. Today Louis is still with Scott and spends much of his time in London and touring with the group. His excellent guitar work with Scott's quartet and also that on his own recent solo and duo albums, establishes him as one of the few top jazz guitarists outside the U.S.A. today.

SELECTED RECORDS

'Louis the First'	Hawk Jazz	Shalp 147
'Baubles, Bangles and Beads'	Wave	LP12
'Out on his Own'	Livia	LRLP 1
'Louis Stewart'	Pye	NSPL 18555

SELECTED READING

'Louis Stewart'	Jeffrey Pike, 'Guitar', January 1975

Gabor Szabo

COURTESY CRESCENDO/PHOTO ALAN S. FLOOD

GABOR SZABO

Born—Budapest, Hungary

8th March 1936

Gabor Szabo received his first guitar as a gift from his father when he was 14. For four years he explored the instrument and taught himself to play with such success, that from 1954—6 he was not only playing professionally with various groups in Budapest, but he was also writing music for films and radio.

He gained a knowledge of jazz through records and the radio. On 22nd November 1956 he left Hungary as he was a freedom fighter during the revolution, and arrived as a refugee in the U.S.A. He was fortunate to become a pupil at the Berklee School of Jazz from 1957—9, and he gained popularity gigging with bands such as the one led by Japanese pianist Toshiko.

From 1961 for four years, Szabo gained prominence in the Chico Hamilton quartet and in late 1965 he was featured in the Charles Lloyd Quartet. In 1964 'Downbeat' voted him 'The best new jazz guitarist' jointly with Atilla Zoller and from 1966—8 he fronted his own group. A change in the style of his playing began in 1969 as he seemed to be strongly influenced by the blues, eastern music, and also heavy rock.

In recent years Gabor has been based in Los Angeles working successfully with different groups and in television. The latest of his groups entitled 'The Perfect Circle' has a repertoire ranging from pseudo classical music to hard rock. Szabo continues to innovate and investigate new approaches to music and he is currently a guitarist who successfully appeals to both jazz and popular audiences.

SELECTED RECORDS

'Chico Hamilton—Passin' Thru' '	Impulse	A29
'The Sorcerer'	Impulse	M1PL 506
'Gypsy 66'	Impulse	A 9105
'Spellbinder'	Impulse	A 9123
'The California Dreamers'	Impulse	9151
'Blowin' some old Smoke'	Buddah	BDS 2051L
'Magical Connection'	Blue Thumb	BTS 23
'Jazz Raga'	Impulse	A 9128
'Greatest Hits'	Impulse	AS 9204—2
'Faces'	Mercury	SRM 1—1141

SELECTED READING

'Gabor Szabo—The Changing Times'	Don De Michael, 'Downbeat' 5th October 1967
'Szabo'	Interview—'Guitar Player', December 1969
'Returning to Hungary'	Frankie Nemko, 'Guitar Player', July 1975

TOOTS THIELEMANS

Born—JEAN THIELEMANS
Brussels, Belgium

29th April 1922

Toots Thielemans

Known throughout the world as the most brilliant harmonica player in jazz, 'Toots' Thielemans is also a very fine jazz guitarist.

In 1941 Thielemans who was then a mathematics student, heard some Django Reinhardt records. These led him to teach himself to play the guitar and by 1944 he had already played in U.S. Army clubs. Although he had visited the United States in 1947 it was not until 1951 that he decided to settle in America. His decision probably came after a successful tour with the Benny Goodman sextet in 1950 which helped establish him in the U.S.A. He was offered the guitar seat with the George Shearing quintet in 1953 a position he held until 1959. The following year he formed his own group.

In the mid-nineteen sixties he was a staff musician in New York City, and he was to work in the studios until 1969 when he worked on several projects with bandleader/composer Quincy Jones. With his own quartet Toots toured Russia in 1972 and then continued a successful musical career both in Europe and the U.S.A.

Toots Thielemans' guitar style is instantly recognizable as he often whistles and hums in unison with his own guitar improvisations, much in the manner of bassist Slam Stewart. He is also a very able composer, his most famous compositions being the popular 'Bluesette' and the background music for the U.S. television series 'Sesame Street'.

SELECTED RECORDS

'Too Much! Toots'	Philips	PHM 200—188
'The Whistler and his Guitar'	ABC Paramount	ABC 482
'Time Out for Toots'	Decca	9204
'Captured Alive'	Choice	CR 1007
'Spotlight on Toots'	Polydor	2484055

SELECTED READING

'From Europe to America—Jean Thielemans'	Ken Meier, 'Downbeat', 24th July 1958
'Triple Threat—Toots Thielemans'	'Downbeat', 25th November 1971

RENE THOMAS

Born—Liege, Belgium
25th February 1927

Died—Santander, Spain, 3rd January 1975

Rene Thomas with Stan Getz.

René Thomas began studying the guitar at the age of 10, and was mainly self taught. He started professionally on the guitar freelancing in Belgium and France, and first gained prominence playing with visiting American jazz musicians in Paris in 1955, including trumpeter Chet Baker.

He decided to emigrate to Montreal, Canada in 1958 where he was to remain until 1973. He did visit New York in 1958 and recorded with saxophonist Sonny Rollins and pianist Toshiko. This visit made a very great impression on jazz lovers in the New York area.

He toured with tenor saxophonist, Stan Getz from 1969—72 and also made some records with him. From 1973 until his early death in 1975 from a heart attack in Spain, the Belgian guitarist mainly worked in Europe. René Thomas was a fine jazz guitarist whose style was originally influenced by Django Reinhardt and later to a much greater extent by Jimmy Raney, yet still one that retained his own continental individuality.

SELECTED RECORDS

'René Thomas/Bobby Jaspar Quintet'	RCA Victor (Italy)	TML 10324
'Meeting Mr. Thomas'	Barclay	84091
'Guitar Groove'	Jazzland	JL 27
'Song Book in Europe' (with Lucky Thompson)	MPS	15231
'Chet Baker is Back'	RCA (Italy)	RCA 10307

COURTESY ECM RECORDS

Ralph Towner

RALPH TOWNER

Born Chehalis, Washington, U.S.A.

1st March 1940

Regarded as one of the most musically adventurous of the younger jazz guitarists Ralph Towner started playing the guitar at the relatively late age of 22. His early musical education began at the age of three on the piano, his mother being a piano teacher and his father a trumpeter. But it was not until he started at the University of Oregon in 1958 that he devoted serious study to music and his chosen instrument then was the trumpet. It was only in his last year at college that he was attracted to the guitar and from that time he devoted most of his time to an intensive study of the instrument. After leaving the University of Oregon, Towner travelled in 1963 to Vienna, Austria, and studied under the classical guitarist Karl Scheit. After one year of intense study with Scheit, the young guitarist returned to the University of Oregon, to start a master degree. This he did not complete but he returned in 1967 to Vienna for a further year's study with Scheit.

On Towner's return to America this talented multi-instrumentalist settled in New York where he earned his living as a pianist. He worked with artists such as singer Astrud Gilberto and bassist Dave Holland. On one or two occasions he played with Miles Davis and Keith Jarrett. It was in 1970 that he first came to prominence when he joined the Paul Winter consort playing the 12 string guitar, an instrument he now uses on several of his jazz recordings.

He left the consort after two years and formed a new group, a quartet with bassist Glen Moore called 'Oregon'. This group developed a very beautiful and individual sound generated by Towner's intellectual and new approach to music. Since that time each year brings increasing popularity for Towner, including his winning of the 'Downbeat's critics' poll in 1974.

SELECTED RECORDS

'Oregon—Winter Light'	Vanguard	VSD 79350
'Oregon—In Concert'	Vanguard	VSD 79358
'Trios/Solos'	ECM	1025
'Diary'	ECM	1032
'Matchbook'	ECM	1056
'Saragasso Sea' (with John Abercrombie)	ECM	1080
'Solstice, Sounds and Shadows'	ECM	1095

SELECTED READING

'Ralph Towner—A Chorus of Inner Voices'	Charles Mitchell, 'Downbeat', June 19th 1975
'Ralph Towner of Oregon'	Len Lyons, 'Guitar Player', December 1975

Phil Upchurch

COURTESY GUITAR PLAYER

PHIL UPCHURCH

Born—Chicago, Illinois, U.S.A.

19th July 1941

Phil Upchurch

Phil Upchurch originally started on a ukulele given to him at the age of 12 by his father who was a pianist. He changed to guitar when he was 13 and was virtually self taught. He gained a lot of experience on both electric bass and guitar with various Chicago bands.

Upchurch's first real break was when he became accompanist for the Rhythm and Blues singer D. Clark. His work with this artist earned him many other bookings in the Chicago recording studios backing many artists including jazz stars Dizzy Gillespie, Stan Getz and Ramsey Lewis.

Phil was drafted into the Army in 1965 and was based in Germany. During his stay there he had many opportunities to play jazz with various small groups. He left the forces in 1967 and returned to Chicago where his guitar playing was once more much in demand. He continued to back big name jazz stars such as Cannonball Adderley and Grover Washington.

Upchurch toured the U.S.A. in 1970 with pianist Ramsey Lewis and in 1971 tried to settle in California where he worked with Quincey Jones. He also toured Japan with Jones in 1972. Today Phil Upchurch once more lives in Chicago where he is much in demand both as a jazz, and a Rhythm and Blues guitarist for recording and club work.

SELECTED RECORDS

'Feeling Blue'	Milestone	9010
'Darkness, Darkness'	Blue Thumb	BTS 6005
'Upchurch/Tennyson'	Motown Kudu	KU—22—51

SELECTED READING

'Phil Upchurch—Studio Soul'	Dan Morgenstern, 'Downbeat', 26th June 1969
'Jammin' with Phil'	Chuck Mitchell, 'Downbeat', 6th June 1974
'Phil Upchurch'	'Guitar Player', December 1969

COURTESY GUITAR PLAYER

George Van Eps

GEORGE VAN EPS

Born— GEORGE ABEL VAN EPS
Plainfield, New Jersey

7th August 1911

George Van Eps is regarded by most leading guitarists as one of the 'fathers' of the modern plectrum guitar. His harmonies and musical concepts have become a legend over the years.

George Van Eps comes from a very musical family, his father Fred Van Eps was a world-famous banjo star. In fact it was the banjo that George began playing at the age of 12. A bout of rheumatic fever forced him to leave school at 14 and this was when he took up the guitar.

He played with the Smith Ballew band from 1929—31 and the Freddy Martin outfit 1931—3. But his first real break came when he joined the Benny Goodman orchestra in 1934. This brought the attention of the world's jazz lovers to his unique guitar. In 1935 he joined the popular Ray Noble band, an association that lasted on and off until 1941. During this period Van Eps found that many top radio jobs came his way.

During World War Two George left the music profession to help his father, who owned a recording equipment factory in Plainfield, to supply items necessary for the war effort. But by 1944 the master guitarist was once more involved with the Ray Noble band and all types of radio work. He was also strongly featured on many fine records with the Paul Weston orchestra.

Right up to 1961 he was in great demand as a sideman for recording. But in 1961 he opened a model shop in Glendale, California with his wife. Because of his interest in models and the work involved in running the business, Van Eps gave up playing the guitar professionally until 1964. Although he is now virtually semi-retired he still gives occasional concerts and recitals on the seven string guitar, an instrument that he originally designed as early as 1939.

His excellent guitar music and methods, plus his recorded work on the guitar bear witness to his giant ability, and ensure that the name of George Van Eps will always be a legend for all guitarists.

SELECTED RECORDS

'George Van Eps' 1949 (with Eddie Miller)	Jump	12—6
'Carefree' with Paul Weston Orchestra	Capitol	1261
'Solo Mood' with Paul Weston Orchestra	Capitol	CL 879
'Mood for Twelve' with Paul Weston Orchestra	Capitol	CL 693
'Mellow Guitar'	Columbia	929
'Soliloquy'	Capitol	ST 267
'My Guitar'	Capitol	ST 2533
'Seven String Guitar'	Capitol	ST 2783

SELECTED MUSIC

'George Van Eps Method'	Epiphone Music Co.
'George Van Eps 3 Solos'	Epiphone Music Co.
'George Van Eps 6 Solos'	Plymouth Music Co.

SELECTED READING

'Seven Eps'	'Guitar Player', December 1967
'George Van Eps—A Master Guitarist's Reflections'	John Tynan, 'Downbeat', 16th July 1964
'George Van Eps'	Interview, 'Guitar Player', March 1970
'George Van Eps'	Ivor Mairants, 'B.M.G.' September 1970
'George Van Eps'	Ivor Mairants, 'Guitar', April 1974
'George Van Eps' 'The Seven String Guitar'	Gretsch Guitar Co.

Al Viola

COURTESY CRESCENDO/PHOTO DENNIS MATTHEWS

AL VIOLA

Born—ALFONSO ALFRED VIOLA
Brooklyn, New York, U.S.A.

16th June 1919

Al Viola was fortunate in having both his mother and elder brother able amateur musicians on several plectrum instruments. It was the guitar that attracted Al most and he devoted all his spare time to that instrument. Initially it was the guitar style of Kress, McDonough, and Van Eps that were to influence him, but it was the electric guitar of Charlie Christian that had the major impact on the young guitarist. Al was fortunate in that he was able to hear in person the legendary guitarist at Minton's and at other clubs in New York. He also listened to Oscar Moore in person playing with the King Cole Trio at Kelly's Stable, and it was Oscar that supplied Al with his first electric guitar.

In 1941 Al was drafted to the Army but he was fortunate to be assigned to the Camp Kohler band in Sacramento. He played guitar in a trio called 'The Three Sergeants'. The original pianist of this group, Louis Ventrella was replaced by Page Cavanaugh. This new trio was so well received that it continued after the war as the Page Cavanaugh Trio a highly successful vocal/instrumental group from 1947—9.

After leaving this trio Viola has led a very rewarding and varied music career. Most recently he has been accompanying Frank Sinatra but he played with Bobby Troup from 1950—4, Ray Anthony 1955—6 and the Harry James band in 1957.

Based in Los Angeles Al Viola is today much in demand as a top studio musician, when he is not touring the world backing such artists as Sinatra. He has also devoted a lot of time to the study of music including a course in harmony and theory at the California Academy of Music, and also studying the classical guitar.

SELECTED RECORDS

'Guitars'	Liberty	3112
'Imagination'	Liberty	3155
'Solo Guitar'	Mode	121
'Guitar Vol. II'	Liberty	LST 7127
'Alone Again'	Legend	1002
'Guitar Lament'	World Pacific	WP 1408
'The Intimate Miss Christy'	Capitol	T 1953

SELECTED MUSIC

'Guitar Lament'	Leeds Music Corporation

SELECTED READING

'Al Viola'	Frankie Nemko, 'Guitar Player', April 1977

Chuck Wayne

COURTESY JAZZ JOURNAL

CHUCK WAYNE

Born—**CHARLES JAGELKA**
New York City, U.S.A.

27th February 1923

Chuck Wayne originally started on the mandolin and was featured in a Russian style balalaika band. His father was a cabinet maker from Czechoslovakia. It is reputed that when the neck of his mandolin warped Chuck threw it into a furnace and went out to buy a guitar, an instrument which he was to teach and master himself. As a result he is today one of the all time jazz greats on his chosen instrument.

In 1941 Chuck was originally working as a liftman when he played his first real professional engagements with Clarence Profit and Nat Jaffe on 52nd Street. He was drafted into the army in 1942. On leaving the forces in 1944 he began what was to be an illustrious and historic career in jazz. From 1944–6 he played with Joe Marsala. For the next two years he played with a wide variety of jazz outfits including the Woody Herman band. His first world wide recognition came when he joined the George Shearing Quintet in 1949 for a period of three years.

After he left Shearing in 1952 Chuck led his own group in New York City for two years. He then joined singer Tony Bennett as an accompanist until 1957. Like many other jazz guitarists he was lost to the television studios when he joined CBS in 1960. Although he still did occasional jazz work it was not until 1973 that he came back into jazz fully when he formed his unique guitar duo with Joe Puma, playing in jazz clubs in the New York area.

Chuck Wayne also plays the classic guitar and currently still resides in New York. His career is still split between jazz, teaching and session work and he has at this time never really received the fame and recognition that his genuine talents on the jazz guitar deserve.

SELECTED RECORDS

'String Fever'	Vik	LX1093
'The Jazz Guitarist'	Savoy	MG 12077
'Tapestry'	Focus	FM 333
'Morning Mist'	Prestige	7367
'Interactions' (duo with Joe Puma)	Choice	CRS 1004
'Fourmost Guitars'	ABC Paramount	ABC 109
'The Guitar Album'	CBS	67275
'Skyliner'	Progressive	KUX–23G

SELECTED READING

'Chuck Wayne'	Ray Moore, 'Guitar Player', February 1970
'Magical Jazz Duo'	Ray Gogerty, 'Guitar Player', March 1974
'Chuck Wayne'	Ivor Mairants, 'Guitar', November 1974

HY WHITE

Born—HYMAN WHITE
Boston, Massachusetts, U.S.A.

17th December 1915

Hy White

Hy White originally started on the violin at the age of nine but changed to the guitar when he was 16.

When he completed his school career Hy played in and around Boston leading his own band. He also worked with Rollie Rogers and Ted Rolfe before going to New York in 1938. He joined the original Woody Herman band in late 1939, leaving in 1944 to join the Les Brown orchestra.

For many years, from the late forties onwards, Hy White has freelanced around the New York area. He has recorded with the bands of Gene Krupa and the Dorsey Brothers and also with many top singers including Bing Crosby, Doris Day, Frank Sinatra and Pearl Bailey.

Today Hy is still based in the New York area, devoting much of his time to teaching as well as being on call for studio work.

SELECTED RECORDS

'Woody Herman's First Herd'	Joker	SM 3059
'Les Brown Orchestra' 1944—6	Hindsight	HSR 103

SELECTED MUSIC

'Guitar Digest' Hy White	Charling Music Corp.
'Hy White Originals' 10 solos	Chas Colins Music Co.
'Guitar Method' Book 1 Hy White	MCA Music
'Guitar Method' Book 2 Hy White	MCA Music
'Folklore for Guitar' Hy White	MCA Music

JACK WILKINS

Born—Brooklyn, New York, U.S.A.

3rd June 1944

Jack Wilkins

Currently one of the top session guitarists in New York, Jack Wilkins is also a very able jazz guitarist spending many nights of the week in New York's jazz clubs playing with various lineups and often with other guitarists such as Al Gafa and Chuck Wayne.

An able pianist and vibist, Jack started on the guitar at the age of 14. He studied with John Mehegan when he was 18 and also the classical guitarist Rodrigo Riera. Over the last few years he has played as a sideman with many top jazz artists including Stan Getz, Dizzy Gillespie, Earl Hines, and Buddy Rich. He recently recorded his first record as leader on the Mainstream label. Many guitarists feel that Jack Wilkins could well become a major figure in the jazz world over the next few years.

SELECTED RECORDS

'Windows'	Mainstream	MRL 396
'Jack Wilkin's Quartet'	Chiaroscuro	CR 156

COURTESY JACK WILKINS/PHOTO K. ABE

COURTESY JIMMY WYBLE

Jimmy Wyble with Red Norvo.

JIMMY WYBLE

Born—Port Arthur, Texas, U.S.A.

25th January 1922

Jimmy Wyble began to seriously study the guitar when he was 13. By the late nineteen thirties he was playing around Houston with various country style bands, although he was playing some jazz and was greatly influenced by the records of Django Reinhardt and Charlie Christian.

From 1941—2 he was a staff musician for a Houston radio station and in 1944 he joined the famed western swing band led by Bob Wills. His first real involvement in jazz was to come when he moved to Los Angeles in the late nineteen forties. Here he soon established himself in the Los Angeles film studios and although not involved professionally in jazz at that time, he was able to mix with many of the top jazzmen living in California and so gain valuable jazz experience.

His first prominent jazz break came when vibist Red Norvo asked him to take the guitar seat in his group in 1956. This was a position he held for eight years touring with Norvo both in the U.S.A. and abroad. During those eight years he also had the opportunity to do some tours with the Benny Goodman band. Wyble took full advantage of his time with both these top groups to develop his jazz style.

Since 1965 Jimmy has once more been mainly involved in the Los Angeles studios as a top freelance guitarist, working for several television and radio networks as well as films. His main jazz work of recent has been his association with Tony Rizzi's group 'The Five Guitars'.

SELECTED RECORDS

'Jimmy Wyble Quintet—Diane'	Vantage	LP 502
'Classical Jazz'	Jazz Chronicles	JCS 771 and 2
'Wind Jammer—Red Norvo'	Dot	25—126
'Five Guitars Play Charlie Christian'	Milagro	1000
'Jimmy Wyble and Love Bros'	Jazz Chronicles	JCS 773 and 4

SELECTED MUSIC

'Classical/Country'	Playback Publishing Co.

SELECTED READING

'Jimmy Wyble'	Frankie Nemko, 'Guitar Player', June 1977

Bucky Pizzarelli

COURTESY MONMOUTH/EVERGREEN RECORDS

Attila Zoller

COURTESY ENJA RECORDS/PHOTO WOLFGANG FRANKENSTEIN

ATTILA ZOLLER

Born— ATTILA CORNELIUS ZOLLER
Visegrad, Hungary

13th June 1927

Attila Zoller has a strong musical background. His father was a music teacher and conductor and he taught Attila the violin from the age of four. When he was nine Attila also started to play the trumpet and he played this instrument in his school's symphony orchestra for seven years.

When he was almost 18 Zoller went to Budapest to try and become a professional musician. This he realized would be difficult as a trumpeter so he took up the guitar. By 1947 he had made so much progress on the guitar that he was already playing with one of the top commercial bands in Budapest. Realizing that politics were going to make things difficult in Hungary he decided to move to Vienna in 1948. Here he joined up with Vera Auer an accordionist. Their quartet played in a jazz style, and they worked together successfully for five years, Their group won the Combo prize at a 1951 jazz contest held in Vienna, although their usual programme mainly consisted of dance and cabaret music.

By 1954 Attila had decided to devote his career to jazz and he moved to West Germany. He played with pianist Jutta Hipp for a year from 1954 and saxophonist Hans Koller from 1956—9. Whilst he was in Germany he had many valuable opportunities to play with visiting American jazz musicians.

Attila decided to emigrate to the U.S.A. in 1959 and for a while his trip was sponsored by the Framus instrument company. On the recommendation of Jim Hall and John Lewis he then received a scholarship for the Lenox School of Jazz in Massachusetts.

After leaving Lenox, Attila worked for a short while with drummer Chico Hamilton and then in 1962 flautist Herbie Mann asked him to join his group. They worked together successfully for three years and in 1965 Zoller formed his own quartet which was based in New York City.

Attila's guitar style has recently been influenced by jazz/rock and avant garde as his new recordings show. At this time Zoller, a very individual and talented guitarist has been very busy, particularly in Europe, playing in concerts and at jazz clubs, as well as recording. Still based in New York Attila also spends some of his time developing new innovations for musical instruments, including a vibraphone pickup, and also organising guitar clinics.

SELECTED RECORDS

'Legendary Oscar Pettiford'	Black Lion	BLP 30185
'Zo-Ko-Ma'	MPS	15—170
'The Horizon Beyond'	Emarcy	25013
'Gypsy Cry'	Embryo	SD 523
'Dream Bells'	Enja	2078

SELECTED READING

'The Odyssey of Attila Zoller'	Dan Morgenstern, 'Downbeat', July 1965

Dave Goldberg

COURTESY C. E. H. SMITH

THE JAZZ GUITAR

THE OTHER JAZZ GUITARISTS

On the opposite page is a fine action photograph of the late Dave Goldberg. Dave developed a reputation by the mid-nineteen sixties as Britain's foremost jazz guitarist, but tragically died before he could gain full world-wide recognition. No commercial recordings are available today of Goldberg's jazz artistry but those who heard him play, constantly testify to his great ability.

Below and on the next three pages are photographs of some of the many fine guitarists in the world today who are involved with playing jazz on a regular or occasional basis. They are only a few of the many to whom a tribute must be paid. Their devotion and love of both jazz and their chosen instrument contributes in an important way to the general evolution of the guitar in jazz. Many more names could of course be mentioned, Rune Gustafsson of Sweden and Wim Overgaauw of Holland are only two of many fine guitarists that spring to mind, but I believe that the main biographical section of this book has included all those guitarists who have been great innovators or who have made a major contribution to jazz.

Cedric West

COURTESY CSL

COURTESY FAMOUS DOOR RECORDS

Lloyd Ellis

COURTESY GUITAR

Terry Smith

COURTESY GUITAR/PHOTO GEORGE CLINTON

Judd Proctor

218

Billy Mackel

COURTESY JAZZ JOURNAL/PHOTO ERIC H. JELLY

John Scofield

COURTESY ENJA RECORDS

Cal Collins

COURTESY FAMOUS DOOR RECORDS

Diz Disley

Denny Wright

COURTESY GUITAR/PHOTO GEORGE CLINTON

COURTESY GUITAR/PHOTO GEORGE CLINTON

INDEX OF GUITARISTS INCLUDED IN THE

BIOGRAPHICAL SECTION OF 'THE JAZZ GUITAR'

THE JAZZ GUITAR

ITS INSTRUMENTS

THE JAZZ GUITAR

ITS INSTRUMENTS

In a book covering the subject of the evolution of the guitar in jazz and its players, I feel it would be wrong not to mention the actual instruments used by jazz guitarists over the years. The manufacture of steel strung guitars suitable for jazz until recent times has always been dominated by makers in the United States of America. The leader and most important of these has been the Gibson company. To a lesser extent, guitars made by Epiphone (now owned by Gibson), Guild, and C. F. Martin have also been used by jazz players. In more recent times the exclusive hand made guitars of the late John D'Angelico and his successor Jimmy D'Aquisto have been the first choice of many jazz guitarists. There are of course many other American guitar makers, both past and present, Harmony, Stella, Rickenbacker, Fender, Ovation and Gretsch have all been used by guitarists over the years but their popularity for jazz players has been limited. This is in spite of the fact that Rickenbacker and Fender have made valuable contributions to the development of the guitar's electronics.

With the exception of the unique Maccaferri guitar made in France during the thirties, an instrument used almost exclusively over the years by Django Reinhardt and the Hot Club de France, European makers have not made much impact on jazz guitarists. With the incredible rise of the Japanese guitar industry over the last 10 years, two makers, Ibanez and Yamaha, have developed ranges of fine quality guitars which are sold all over the world. At this time Gibson, Guild and Ibanez seem to be the most popular makes of guitars for jazz guitarists.

A brief history of Gibson, C. F. Martin, Epiphone, Guild and Maccaferri is given below.

GIBSON

The Gibson company was originated by Orville H. Gibson (1856–1918). He was born in Chataugay, New York, his father John Gibson had originally emigrated from England. He started as a shoe store assistant in Kalamazoo, Michigan, and he was also a part time instrument maker, working in his own private workshop. It was his original conception

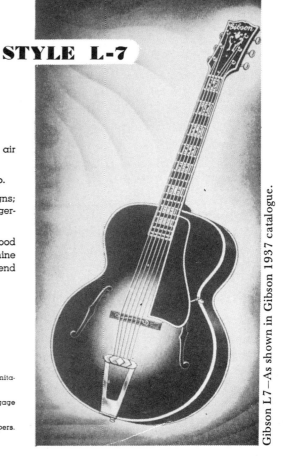

STYLE L-7

Gibson L7 – As shown in Gibson 1937 catalogue.

Advanced Model
CARVED TOP AND BACK

- Body size—17″ wide and 21″ long.

- Northern maple back and rim; mahogany neck; genuine air seasoned spruce top; rosewood fingerboard.

- Chocolate brown finish with golden sunburst shading on top.

- Fingerboard and peghead inlaid with attractive pearl designs; top and bottom edges of body, peghead, fingerboard and finger-rest bound with white ivoroid.

- Elevated brown celluloid fingerrest; side position marks; rosewood adjustable bridge; nickel plated individual Grover machine heads, and new design extension tailpiece; 19 frets; white end pin.

- Exclusive Gibson Adjustable Truss Rod neck construction.

PRICE $125.00

CASES

No. 606 — Strong three ply construction — covered with strong waterproof imitation black leather — purple flannel lining. $18.00.

No. 600 — Covered with heavy waterproof Aeroplane Cloth — sturdy luggage catches — heavy American Beauty silk plush lining. $28.00.

Case Cover: Tan zipper waterproof cover — leather bindings — metal bumpers. $15.00.

that the carved top principle of violin making could be applied to mandolin and guitar making. The results of his experiments were very successful and the reputation of his fine instruments soon spread far and wide. In 1902 he made an agreement with five Kalamazoo businessmen and the Gibson Mandolin-Guitar Mfg. Company was formed.

A vast range of fine guitars, mandolins, harp guitars and later banjos were manufactured by the fast growing Gibson company. In 1920, two years after the death of its founder, Gibson was fortunate to add to their staff the brilliant Lloyd Loar, a fine musician, composer and acoustical engineer. He perfected and developed the original ideas of Orville Gibson in relation to the arch top guitar. The L5 and L7 guitars were his developments and became amongst the most sought after instruments for jazz players for many years to come. Loar left Gibson in 1924 after a dispute over his desire to produce electrically amplified guitars. He then formed the Vivi-Tone Company which produced electric guitars more than a decade before they would become accepted as a legitimate instrument, but he was not commercially successful.

The mid-nineteen thirties saw the development by Gibson of the super 400 and then the first important production electric jazz guitar the ES150, which was used by Charlie Christian, and later by many other jazz guitarists of the time.

In 1944 the now highly successful Gibson company was purchased by the Chicago Musical Instrument Company who enlarged the Gibson factory and over the years many new models were developed and introduced. Electronics, particularly with the help of Les Paul, were improved to a very high level. The Gibson ES175 guitar in particular has for many years been a favourite for jazz guitarists all over the world.

Throughout its long history Gibson has always associated itself with jazz guitarists. In the twenties—Eddie Lang, the thirties Carl Kress and Dick McDonough, and in the fifties and sixties several Gibson guitars bore the names of top jazz artists such as Johnny Smith, Howard Roberts, Tal Farlow, and Barney Kessel. In more recent times Gibson have continued this tradition with developments such as the special acoustic guitar with sitar like drones that it has built for John McLaughlin. The contribution of Gibson to the development of the jazz guitar has been a unique and vital one. The Chicago Musical Instrument company also purchased the Epiphone company in 1957, and since 1974 has been part of Norlin Inc., a concern which distributes a vast range of musical instruments in most countries of the world.

Gibson Super 400

Gibson ES—175D

C. F. MARTIN

C. F. Martin was born in Germany in 1796. He learnt the art of guitar making in Markneukirchen and later in Vienna. He emigrated to New York in 1833 where he made the first American made C. F. Martin guitars in a small workshop.

The business moved to Nazareth, Pennsylvania, in 1839 where it has flourished as a family business right up to the present day.

The Martin guitar is the world's leader in flat top steel strung guitars but it has never been successful in its attempts to make arch top guitars. As a result the Martin guitar has not often been used by jazz guitarists. It has however been a favourite for singer/blues guitarists since the end of the nineteenth century right up to the present day, and as such has made a contribution to jazz.

Martin 000—28

EPIPHONE

The Epiphone company was established by Anastasios Stathopoulo in 1873 in New York. Stathopoulo was a violin maker and luthier of high repute. After the death of its founder the Epiphone company prospered for many years under the management of Epi Stathopoulo and his two brothers. Their range consisted of many guitars, banjos and mandolins not unlike the range being offered at the same time by the Gibson company in Kalamazoo. Top guitarists of the thirties, certainly regarded the Epiphone arch top guitar as an equal to Gibson.

With the advent of the electric guitar the Gibson company took the initiative and strode ahead of Epiphone, finally purchasing the latter company in 1957 after the death of Epi Stathopoulo. Many of Epiphone's top craftsmen left and joined the then recently formed Guild company. In the last few years the Epiphone guitar range has been made in Japan for Norlin Inc.

Epiphone Broadway

GUILD

The Guild company was founded in New York City in 1952 by Alfred Dronge a former professional guitarist and music shop owner. He started with five guitar makers, two of whom had been top men with Epiphone. Over the next few years the Guild company under Dronge's demanding supervision built up a fine reputation. It also gained several more of the Epiphone company's expert craftsmen in 1957 when Epiphone was purchased by C.M.I. In 1956 Guild moved to Hoboken, New Jersey and continued to expand its production under the guidance of its founder Albert Dronge, who ensured that the quality of his guitars was of the highest standard.

Today Guild is a division of Avnet Inc. a public company with diverse interests, and its guitars are made in a new factory at Westerly, Rhode Island. Within a relatively short period of time the Guild company has developed a world-wide reputation for its guitars, and its jazz guitars are without a doubt some of the finest being made today.

Guild Artist Award

D'ANGELICO AND D'AQUISTO

John D'Angelico was born in 1905 and was originally a violin maker. Using the Gibson L5 guitar as his model he opened in 1932 a workshop on Manhattan's Lower East Side making quality hand made guitars. The reputation of his fine instruments earned him orders from many of the top players in the New York area. D'Angelico tragically died in 1964 but he had fortunately passed his great knowledge on to his young apprentice Jimmy D'Aquisto who had joined him in 1952.

Jimmy D'Aquisto today has a fine guitar workshop in Farmingdale, New York. He is recognized throughout the world as the foremost arch top guitar maker and he has added many of his own ideas to those learnt from D'Angelico. He 'tailors' his magnificent guitars for each individual player's requirements. As a result his instruments are highly prized with a waiting list of up to three years for them and a price tag of several thousand dollars.

D'Aquisto New Yorker

228

MACCAFERRI

Mario Maccaferri was born in 1900 in Cento near Bologna, Italy. As a young man he was not only a brilliant instrument maker but also a classical guitarist of concert standard. He felt that he could apply some of the principles of construction of other instruments to the guitar and when he was in London in the late twenties he showed his ideas to the directors of Selmer of London. They were so impressed they immediately recommended him to Selmer of Paris. The result was a three year association beginning in 1930 between Maccaferri and Selmer. During these three years Maccaferri controlled the production of his guitars in Selmer's Paris factory which he himself had designed for them.

Within a short time these distinctive and beautiful instruments were to be one of the most popular guitars in Europe for dance band and jazz guitarists, the most famous being Django Reinhardt and the members of his group the quintet of the Hot Club de France. After a dispute in 1933 Maccaferri left Selmer who continued producing the guitar. They changed the 'D' sound hole to a

Selmer/Maccaferri Factory, Paris, France 1931

Mario Maccaferri (left) and Harry Volpe testing plastic jazz guitars.

small oval hole and also made the neck 14 frets clear of the body instead of 12. But the production of all models ceased at the end of the thirties.

Maccaferri himself continued to have a long and successful career in other trades. He left for the U.S.A. in 1939 where he applied his great engineering skills to the plastics industry. His love for the guitar has always remained and he even at one time tried to make a range of professional guitars, including electric guitars, out of plastic. Although over $100,000 was invested in the project, it was eventually abandoned.

In the last few years Mario Maccaferri has got together with British guitar distributors, Summerfields of Gateshead, and guitars of his original nineteen thirty design are now being made again in Japan under the CSL brand. These instruments are proving extremely popular, particularly amongst followers of the music of Django Reinhardt.

There are several excellent books and articles which deal in detail with the fascinating subject of the history and construction of guitars, including of course those instruments used by jazz artists. Some of these books are listed below.

CSL/Maccaferri

COURTESY CSL

SELECTED READING

'The History of the American Guitar'	Ken Achard. Music New Services 1978
'The Guitar Book'	Tom Wheeler. Harper & Row 1974
'The Electric Guitar'	Donald Brosnac. Panjandrum 1975
'Guitars'	Tom and Ann Mary Evans. Paddington 1977
'The Gibson Story'	Julius Bellson. Gibson Co. 1973
'Martin Guitars'	Mike Longworth. Colonial Press 1975
'Steel String Guitar Construction'	Irving Sloane. Dutton 1975
'The Rebirth of Django's Guitar'	M. J. Summerfield. CSL Co. 1978
'John D'Angelico'	Richard Hetrick. 'Guitar Player', January 1973

Also recommended are reprints of various pre-war Gibson, Epiphone and Martin Guitar catalogues, available from Picking Productions, 545 Madison Avenue, New York, NY 10022, U.S.A.

DJANGO REINHARDT

"LE ROI DE LA GUITARE"

RETOUR DE LONDRES, OU IL A OBTENU
UN SUCCÈS SANS PRÉCÉDENT
AVEC SA GUITARE FRANÇAISE

Studio Tronchet

...car c'est
une

Example of Selmer Advert for the Maccaferri Guitar—mid-nineteen thirties.

Creative Guitar

The sound of Howard Roberts and his Epiphone guitar is the unique and inventive sound of one of America's most creative musicians.

Steeped in the traditional jazz idiom and a first-call sideman for dozens of top recording stars, Howard has forged a new, completely different sound of his own that is explorative, yet unpretentious—fiery and hard-swinging, but creative. And underscoring every note is the earthy honesty of the artist himself.

For all his solo and studio work and for his own Capitol recordings, Howard plays Epiphone, a guitar that guarantees him superb sensitivity, excellent response and a beautifully dependable performance *every* time.

the choice of those who can hear the difference

EPIPHONE

Epiphone guitars and amplifiers are products of CMI, 7373 N. Cicero, Lincolnwood, Ill.

GEORGE BENSON
THE GEORGE BENSON QUARTET

George Benson's Amp is a Guild ThunderBird. It cuts right through organ in his quartet.

Guild

Guitarist, composer, singer, leader of his own hard-driving jazz quartet — George Benson! □ "A young guitarist with roots in Charlie Christian", said Down Beat. □ "Most exciting new guitarist on the jazz scene today", said the album caption for his first LP record. □ "Simmering, steaming, boiling . . . always cooking", said the liner notes for his second. □ George Benson has been playing Guild ever since he was 17. Which really hasn't been very long at all. For Catalog No. 7054-B, write Guild Musical Instruments, Hoboken, New Jersey 07030. Or see your music dealer now.

A DIVISION OF AVNET, INC.

Hear artist MARY OSBORNE and her Gretsch "White Falcon" on the Jack Sterling Show (WCBS—New York)

On Stage—And Great!

The first note...voices hush...you are being watched, listened to, appreciated. Your talent and showmanship have paid off. So have the terrific sound and looks of your Gretsch guitar!

Have you seen and played the famous Gretsch "White Falcon" electric guitar? It's a real showpiece...now available in a new Super Project-O-Sonic electronic model (stereo sound, with two amps, at *playing level*). Well worth a special trip to your dealer's. Ask him to make one available for you, soon. Today, write for Gretsch's completely detailed Project-O-Sonic folder and complete guitar catalog.

GRETSCH THE FRED. GRETSCH MFG. CO. • Dept. D-24G • 60 BROADWAY, B'KLYN 11, N.Y.

FREDDIE GREEN of the Count Basie Band

Reputation Reflected

A guitarist's ability; what others think of his playing, determine how far he will go. Choice of instrument is important. Freddie Green plays a Gretsch guitar. So do a growing number of successful guitarists, like him.

If success is important to you, consider a Gretsch : guitar sound like no other...modern styling and playing features you won't find elsewhere. Whether you play Acoustic or Electromatic guitar, Gretsch has a model for you. Try one out at your dealer's soon. Today, write for Gretsch's detailed guitar catalog.

GRETSCH THE FRED GRETSCH MFG. CO., • DEPT M-109   60 BROADWAY B'KLYN 11, N.Y.

Examples of Epiphone/Guild/Gretsch adverts from 1950's/60's featuring jazz guitarists.

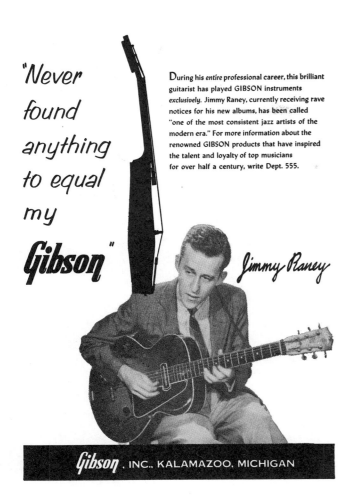

"Never found anything to equal my *Gibson*"

Jimmy Raney

During his *entire* professional career, this brilliant guitarist has played GIBSON instruments *exclusively*. Jimmy Raney, currently receiving rave notices for his new albums, has been called "one of the most consistent jazz artists of the modern era." For more information about the renowned GIBSON products that have inspired the talent and loyalty of top musicians for over half a century, write Dept. 555.

Gibson, INC., KALAMAZOO, MICHIGAN

"Gibson Boy"...Tal Farlow

Truly a booster of his favorite guitar, Tal Farlow has written and recorded "Gibson Boy" in a newly released album. Heralded as the "brightest new star" among guitarists, Tal justifies this title in his brilliant recordings, his enthusiastic jazz sessions. For his fresh easy style, his wide ranges of moods and music, Tal Farlow is a confirmed "Gibson-ite," as are so many other top stars.

GIBSON, INC., Kalamazoo, Michigan

BARNEY KESSEL Guitar

Barney Kessel means guitar to a great many people. A jazz guitar . . . a guitar with individual sounds . . . a guitar with a highly personal technique . . . a guitar that makes you feel you've experienced something very special after you've heard it played. It's the magic of this guitar which gives Barney his perennial position at the top of the popularity polls. Barney is one of the most inventive and vital musicians in jazz . . . as a soloist, in a combo, with a big-name band. Whether he's playing a concert in Paris or Venezuela, packing them in at Chicago's London House and Hollywood's Sanbah, or working (and directing) a network TV show, Barney's breathtaking creativity on the guitar produces reverent awe and loud acclaim. The sudden chord changes, distinctive tunes and dramatically varied harmonics are uniquely Barney Kessel guitar. And by the way, did you know that there are now available two Barney Kessel Model instruments . . created by *Gibson*

Gibson, Inc., Kalamazoo, Michigan

the Incredible Jazz Guitar of

Wes Montgomery

"...whatever he does comes alive, the mark of a true artist"

A self-taught master of the jazz guitar, until recently Wes had done all of his playing (except for two years with Lionel Hampton) in and around his native Indianapolis. He didn't cut his first record album until late in 1959.

But the Montgomery sound had long been known and respected among professional musicians. And, once "discovered," the news of this man from Indiana spread to jazz enthusiasts everywhere.

What is the Montgomery sound? It's an exciting quality that makes Montgomery music come alive. It's a terrific swing, the ability to build solos dramatically, to climax after climax. A sense of rightness. A smooth, easy, flowing style. It's the sound of great jazz . . . from a guitar.

Most of all . . . the Montgomery sound is a soft, delicate, exceedingly sensitive kind of music that is created deep within his being. Yes, Wes Montgomery plays a truly incredible jazz guitar. And his guitar is a *Gibson*

Gibson, Inc. Kalamazoo, Michigan

Examples of Gibson advert from 1950's/60's featuring jazz guitarists.

Promotion photograph of George Benson with the two Ibanez jazz guitars he has designed.

SOURCES OF INFORMATION
AND SUPPLIES

JAZZ AND GUITAR MAGAZINES

*'Downbeat'
222 W. Adams Street
Chicago 11 60606
U.S.A.

*'Crescendo'
122 Wardour Street
London,
England

'Jazz Down Under'
Box 202
Camden NSW. 2570
Australia

'Guitar Player'
Box 615
Saratoga
CA 95070
U.S.A.

'Cadence Magazine'
RT 1 Box 345
Redwood
N.Y. 13679
U.S.A.

'Jazz Circle News'
8 St. James Square
Manchester 2
England

'Pickin'
North American Cue Building
545 Madison Avenue
New York NY10022
U.S.A.

'Jazz Hot'
14 Rue Chaptal
75009 Paris
France

'Jazz Journal'
7 Carnaby Street
London W1V 1PG
England

*'Coda'
Box 87
Station J
Toronto
Ontario M4J 4XB
Canada

'Jazz Forum'
Postfach 671
AH011 Wien
Austria

'Guitar Magazine'
20 Denmark Street
London WC2H 8NE
England

'Vintage Jazz Mart'
4 Hillcrest gardens
Dollis Hill
London NW2 6HZ
England

'Melody Maker'
24—34 Meymott Street
London SE1 9LU
England

'Jazz Podium'
Vogelsangstrasse 32
7000 Stuttgart 1
West Germany

*Also supply good selection of jazz books, methods and music by mail. Lists available on application.

JAZZ RECORD AND BOOK SHOPS

ENGLAND

Bloomsbury Book Shop
31—5 Great Ormond Street
London WC1N 3HZ

Dobell's Jazz Record Shop
77 Charing Cross Road
London WC2

Collett's Record Shop
108 Shaftesbury Avenue
London WC2

Books and Magazines
New and Second Hand

Records, Books and Magazines
New and Second Hand

Records, Books and Magazines
New and Second Hand

Ivor Mairants Music Centre 56 Rathbone Place London W1P 1AB	Guitars—New and Second Hand Books and Music—New
Foyles Charing Cross Road London W1	Books and Music—New
Dave Carey's Swing Shop 1B Mitcham Lane Streatham London SW16	Records—New
H.M.V. Shop 363 Oxford Street London W1R 2BJ	Records—New
Chappells 20 New Bond Street London W1	Records, Books and Music—New Guitars—New and Second Hand
All Change Records 20 Baker Street London W1	Records—New and Second Hand
Guy Norris Ltd 47 Neal Street London	Records—New and Second Hand
James Asman's Jazz Centre 3A New Row St. Martin's Lane London WC2	Records—New and Second Hand
Pete Russell's Hot Record Stores Ltd 22—24 Market Avenue Plymouth PL1 1PJ	Records—New and Second Hand Books and Magazines—New
J. G. Windows Central Arcade Newcastle upon Tyne	Records, Music and Guitars—New

WEST GERMANY

Berklee Publications D 8000 Munchen 71 Postfach 710 267	Jazz Guitar Music, Methods and Books Extensive Mail Order List available on request
Phonohaus Rossmarket 7 Frankfurt	Records—New

FRANCE

Disques Et Musique 165 Rue de Rennes 75006, Paris	Records—New and Second Hand
Champs Disques 84 Champs Elysees Paris	Records—New

U.S.A.

New York Jazz Museum 236 West 54th Street New York	Records, Books and Magazines—New
King Carol's 111 West 42nd Street and 1500 Broadway at 43rd Street New York	Records—New

Sam Goody's 1290 Avenue of the Americas New York	Records—New
Record Hunter 507 Fifth Avenue New York 10017	Records—New
Rose Discount Record Store 165 West Madison Chicago	Records—New
Manny's 156 West 48th Street New York	Guitars and Music
Sam Ash 160 West 48th Street New York	Guitars and Music

JAZZ RECORD AND BOOK AUCTIONS—*BY MAIL ONLY*

Gary Alderman P.O. Box 9164 Madison WI 53715 U.S.A.	Records and Books
Jeff Barr P.O. Box 7785 Van Nuys, CA 91409 U.S.A.	Records—Second Hand
Leon Leavitt 824¼ North Las Palmas Avenue Los Angeles California 90038 U.S.A.	Records—Second Hand
Brian J. O'Flaherty P.O. Box 5892 San Francisco C.A. 94101 U.S.A.	Records—Second Hand
Wm. Carraro 25 Aberdeen Street Malverne New York 11565 U.S.A.	Records—Second Hand
Mole Jazz 14 Cornwall Road Harpenden Herts AL5 4TH England	Records—New and Second Hand
The Stars of Jazzette Roland Fournier 43 Rue de Etats Gereraux 78000 Versaille France	Records—New
Jubilia Hopp GMBH P.O. Box 23 D7152 Aspach West Germany	Records—New
Rare Records 1R Exchange Suite 310 22030 Sherman Way Canoga Park CA 91314 U.S.A.	Records—New and Second Hand

JAZZ GUITAR SOLOS AND METHODS

Listed below are recommended music publications for jazz guitar which have not already been listed in the players' biographical sections.

'George M. Smith Method'	'Guitarist's Publications—U.S.A.
'Guitar Patterns for Improvisation'	William Fowler, 'Downbeat' Publications
'Jazz Guitar Phrases and Solos'	Bill Pitman, Gwyn Publishing
'Contemporary Jazz Guitar Solos'	Paul Visvader—U.S.A.
'Forty Years of Jazz Guitar'	Don Roberts—Robbins Music
'Jazz Guitar Volumes 1—4'	Warren Nunes—Hansen Music
'Solo Chords'	Roger Hutchinson—REH Publications
'Rhythm Chord System'	Mel Bay Publications
'Jazz Guitar Vols. 1 and 2'	Ronny Lee—Mel Bay Publications
'Guitar Improvising Vols. 1 and 2'	Mel Bay Publications
'A Modern Method for Guitars' Volumes 1—3	Berklee Press Publications

JAZZ GUITAR COURSES

Berklee College of Music, 1140 Boylston Street, Boston, MA 02215, U.S.A.
Guitar Institute of Technology, 1438 North Gower, Hollywood, CA 90028, U.S.A.
Barney Kessel Seminar—The Effective Guitarist for information write Summerfield, Gateshead NE8 3AJ, United Kingdom.

Scenes from a 1976 Barney Kessel Seminar—'The Effective Guitarist'.